cook's library

Quick
& Easy

cook's library

Quick
& Easy

p

This is a Parragon Book
This edition published in 2003

Parragon
Queen Street House
4 Queen Street
Bath BA1 1HE, UK

ISBN: 0-75258-752-8

Printed in China

NOTE

This book uses metric and imperial measurements. Follow the same
units of measurement throughout; do not mix metric and imperial.
All spoon measurements are level: teaspoons are assumed to be 5 ml,
and tablespoons are assumed to be 15 ml. Unless otherwise stated,
milk is assumed to be full fat, eggs and individual vegetables such as
potatoes are medium, and pepper is freshly ground black pepper.

The times given for each recipe are an approximate guide only because the preparation
times may differ according to the techniques used by different
people and the cooking times may vary as a result of the type of oven used.
The preparation times include chilling and marinating times, where appropriate.

Recipes using raw or very lightly cooked eggs should be
avoided by infants, the elderly, pregnant women, convalescents,
and anyone suffering from an illness.

Contents

6   introduction

18   soups

40   snacks & starters

62   fish & seafood

84   meat dishes

102   poultry

118   pasta & rice

158   puddings & desserts

174   index

Introduction

This book is designed to appeal to anyone who wants a wholesome but quick and easy diet, and includes many recipes suitable for vegetarians and vegans. Its main aim is to show people that, with a little forethought, it is possible to spend very little time in the kitchen while still enjoying appetizing food.

The recipes collected together come from all over the world; some of the Indian and barbecue dishes featured require marinating, often overnight, but it is worth remembering that their actual cooking time is very short once the marinade has been absorbed.

The more exotic dishes on offer are balanced by some traditional dishes, which are sure to become firm family favourites. If you want fast food for everyday meals, or you are short on time and want to prepare a tasty dinner party treat, there is something for everybody in this book. To save time in the kitchen, always make sure that you have a stock of staple foodstuffs such as rice, pasta, spices and herbs, so that you can easily turn your hand to any number of these recipes.

Ingredients

Grains and Rice

A good variety of grains is essential. For rice, choose from long-grain, basmati, Italian arborio, short-grain and wild rice. Look out for fragrant Thai rice, jasmine rice and combinations of different varieties to add colour and texture to your dishes. When choosing your rice, remember that brown rice is a better source of vitamin B_1 and fibre. Other grains add variety to the diet. Try to include some barley, millet, bulghur wheat, polenta, oats, semolina, sago and tapioca.

Pasta

Pasta is very popular nowadays, and there are many types and shapes to choose from. Keep a good selection, such as basic lasagne sheets, tagliatelle or fettuccine and spaghetti. For a change, sample some of the many fresh pastas now available. Better still, make your own – handrolling pasta can be very satisfying, and you can buy a special machine for rolling the dough and cutting certain shapes.

Noodles

The Chinese use several varieties of noodle. You will probably find it easier to use the readily available dried varieties, such as egg noodles, which are yellow, rice stick noodles, which are white and very fine, or transparent noodles, which are opaque when dry and turn transparent on cooking. However, cellophane or rice noodles may be used instead.

Pulses

Pulses are a valuable source of protein, vitamins and minerals. Stock up on soya beans, haricot beans, red kidney beans, cannellini beans, chick-peas, lentils, split peas and butter beans. Buy dried pulses for soaking and cooking yourself, or canned varieties for speed and convenience.

Tofu

This soya bean paste is available in several forms. The cake variety, which is soft and spongy and a white-grey colour, is used in this book. It is very bland, but adds texture to dishes and is perfect for absorbing all the other flavours in the dish.

Herbs

A good selection of herbs is important for adding variety to your cooking. Fresh herbs are preferable to dried, but it is essential to have dried ones in stock as a useful back-up. You should store dried thyme, bay leaves, oregano, rosemary, mixed herbs and bouquet garni.

Chinese Five-spice Powder

An aromatic blend of cinnamon, cloves, star anise, fennel and brown peppercorns. It is often used in marinades.

Szechuan Pepper

This is quite hot and spicy and should be used sparingly. It is red in colour and is available from most large supermarkets.

Star Anise

This is an eight-pointed, star-shaped pod with a strong aniseed flavour. The spice is also available ground. If a pod is added to a dish, it should be removed before serving.

Chillies

These come both fresh and dried and in many varieties. The 'hotness' varies so use with caution. The heat is contained in the seeds and membrane and are often discarded. Chilli powder should always be used sparingly. Check whether the powder is pure chilli or a chilli seasoning or blend, which should be milder.

Nuts and Seeds

As well as adding protein, vitamins and useful fats to the diet, nuts and seeds add important flavour and texture to vegetarian meals. Make sure you keep a good supply of nuts such as hazelnuts, pine kernels and walnuts. Coconut is useful too. For your seed collection, have sesame, sunflower, pumpkin and poppy. Pumpkin seeds in particular are a good source of zinc.

Pak Choi

It is also known as Chinese cabbage, and has a mild, slightly bitter flavour.

Bamboo Shoots

These are added for texture, as they have little flavour. Available in cans, they are a very common ingredient in Chinese cooking.

Bean sprouts

These are mung bean shoots, which are very nutritious, containing many vitamins. They add crunch to a recipe and are widely available. Do not overcook them, or they will wilt.

Dried Fruits

Currants, raisins, sultanas, dates, apples, apricots, figs, pears, peaches, prunes, paw-paws, mangoes, figs, bananas and pineapples can all be purchased dried and can be used in lots of different recipes. When buying dried fruits, look for untreated varieties: for example, buy figs that have not been rolled in sugar, and choose unsulphured apricots, if they are available.

Oils and Fats

Oils are useful for adding subtle flavourings to foods, so it is a good idea to have a selection in your storecupboard. Use a light olive oil for cooking and extra virgin olive oil for salad dressings. Use sunflower oil as a good general-purpose oil. Sesame oil is wonderful in stir-fries; hazelnut and walnut oils are superb in salad dressings. Oils and fats add flavour to foods, and contain the important fat-soluble vitamins A, D, E and K. Remember that all fats and oils are high in calories, and that oils are higher in calories than butter or margarine.

Sesame Oil

This is made from roasted sesame seeds and has an intense flavour. It burns easily and is therefore added at the end of cooking for taste, and is not used for frying your recipes.

Chinese Rice Wine

This is similar to dry sherry in colour, alcohol content and smell. It is worth buying Chinese rice wine for its distinctive flavour.

Vinegars

Choose three or four vinegars – red or white wine, cider, light malt, tarragon, sherry or balsamic vinegar, to name just a few. Each will add its own character.

Rice Vinegar

This has a mild, sweet taste that is quite delicate. It is available in some large supermarkets, but if unavailable, use cider vinegar instead.

Mustards

Mustards are made from black, brown or white mustard seeds, which are ground and mixed with spices. Meaux mustard is made from mixed mustard seeds and has a grainy texture with a warm taste. Dijon mustard, made from husked and ground mustard seeds, has a sharp flavour. Its versatility in salads and with barbecues makes it ideal for vegetarians. German mustard is mild and is best used in both Scandinavian and German dishes and American mustard is also mild and quite sweet. English mustard is quite hot and is used with beef and ham.

Bottled Sauces

Teriyaki sauce gives an authentic Japanese flavour to stir-fries. Black bean and yellow bean sauces add an instant authentic Chinese flavour to stir-fries.

Soy Sauce

This is widely available, but it is worth buying a good grade of sauce. Soy sauce is produced in both light and dark varieties – the former is used with fish and vegetables for a lighter colour and flavour, while the latter, being darker, richer, saltier and more intense, is used as a dipping sauce or with strongly flavoured meats.

Using Spices

You can use spices whole, ground, roasted, fried or mixed with yogurt to marinate meat and poultry. One spice can alter the flavour of a dish and a combination of several can produce different colours and textures. The quantities of spices shown in the recipes are merely a guide. Increase or decrease them as you wish, especially in the cases of salt and chilli powder, which are a matter of taste. Many of the recipes in this book call for ground spices, which are generally available in supermarkets as well as in Asian grocers. In India whole spices are ground at home, and there is no doubt that freshly ground spices make a noticeable difference to the taste.

Some recipes require roasted spices. In India, this is done on a *thawa*, but you can use a heavy, ideally cast-iron frying-pan. No water or oil is needed: the spices are simply dry-roasted whole while the pan is shaken to stop them burning on the base of the pan.

Remember that long cooking over a lowish heat will improve the taste of the food as it allows the spices to be absorbed. This is why reheating dishes the following day is no problem for most Indian food.

Basic Recipes

These recipes form the basis of several of the dishes contained throughout this book. Many of these basic recipes can be made in advance and stored for 2 days in the refrigerator or until required.

Basic Tomato Sauce

2 tbsp olive oil
1 small onion, chopped
1 garlic clove, chopped
400 g/14 oz canned chopped tomatoes
2 tbsp chopped fresh parsley
1 tsp dried oregano
2 bay leaves
2 tbsp tomato purée
1 tsp sugar
salt and pepper

1 Heat the olive oil in a saucepan over a medium heat. Add the onion and fry for about 2–3 minutes, or until translucent. Add the garlic and fry for 1 minute.

2 Stir in the tomatoes with their juice, parsley, oregano, bay leaves, tomato purée and sugar. Season to taste with salt and pepper.

3 Bring the sauce to the boil, then simmer for 15–20 minutes, or until the sauce has reduced by half. Taste and adjust the seasoning, if necessary. Remove the bay leaves and discard just before serving.

Béchamel Sauce

300 ml/10 fl oz pint milk
2 bay leaves
3 cloves
1 small onion
55 g/2 oz butter
40 g/1½ oz flour
300 ml/10 fl oz single cream
large pinch of freshly grated nutmeg
salt and pepper

1 Pour the milk into a saucepan and add the bay leaves. Press the cloves into the onion, add to the pan and bring the milk to the boil over a medium heat. Remove the pan from the heat, cover and cool.

2 Strain the milk into a heatproof jug and rinse out the pan. Melt the butter in the pan over a low heat, then stir in the flour. Stir for 1 minute, then gradually pour in the milk, stirring constantly. Cook for 3 minutes, then pour in the cream and bring to the boil over a medium heat. Remove from the heat and season to taste with nutmeg, salt and pepper.

Cheese Sauce

25 g/1 oz butter
1 tbsp flour
250 ml/9 fl oz milk
2 tbsp single cream
pinch of freshly grated nutmeg
40 g/1½ oz freshly grated mature Cheddar cheese
1 tbsp freshly grated Parmesan cheese
salt and pepper

1 Melt the butter in a saucepan over a low heat. Stir in the flour and cook for 1 minute, then gradually pour in the milk, stirring constantly. Stir in the cream and season to taste with nutmeg, salt and pepper.

2 Cook the sauce for 5 minute, then remove from the heat and stir in the cheeses. Stir until the cheeses have melted and blended into the sauce, adjust seasoning and serve or use as required.

Espagnole Sauce

2 tbsp butter

25 g/1 oz plain flour

1 tsp tomato purée

250 ml/9 fl oz hot veal stock

1 tbsp Madeira

1½ tsp white wine vinegar

2 tbsp olive oil

25 g/1 oz bacon, diced

25 g/1 oz carrot, diced

25 g/1 oz onion, diced

15 g/½ oz celery, diced

15 g/½ oz leek, sliced

15 g/½ oz fennel, diced

1 fresh thyme sprig

1 bay leaf

1 Melt the butter in a saucepan over a low heat. Add the flour and cook, stirring constantly, until lightly coloured. Add the tomato purée, then stir in the hot stock, Madeira and white wine vinegar and cook for 2 minutes.

2 Heat the oil in a separate pan over a medium heat. Add the bacon, carrot, onion, celery, leek, fennel, thyme sprig and bay leaf and fry until the vegetables have softened. Remove the vegetables with a slotted spoon and drain. Add the vegetables to the sauce and simmer for 4 hours, stirring occasionally. Strain the sauce before using.

Ragu Sauce

3 tbsp olive oil

40 g/1½ oz butter

2 large onions, chopped

4 celery sticks, sliced thinly

175 g/6 oz streaky bacon, chopped

2 garlic cloves, chopped

500 g/1 lb 2 oz minced lean beef

2 tbsp tomato purée

1 tbsp flour

400 g/14 oz canned chopped tomatoes

150 ml/5 fl oz beef stock

150 ml/5 fl oz red wine

2 tsp dried oregano

½ tsp freshly grated nutmeg

salt and pepper

1 Heat the oil and butter in a small saucepan over a medium heat. Add the onions, celery and bacon and fry for 5 minutes, stirring.

2 Stir in the garlic and minced beef and cook, stirring until the meat has lost its redness. Reduce the heat and cook for 10 minutes, stirring constantly.

3 Increase the heat to medium, stir in the tomato purée and flour and cook for 1–2 minutes. Stir in the tomatoes, stock and wine, then bring to the boil, stirring constantly. Season to taste with salt and pepper and stir in the oregano and nutmeg. Cover and simmer for 45 minutes, stirring. The sauce is now ready to use.

Italian Red Wine Sauce

150 ml/5 fl oz beef stock

150 ml/5 fl oz Espagnole Sauce (see left)

125 ml/4 fl oz red wine

2 tbsp red wine vinegar

4 tbsp shallots, chopped

1 bay leaf

1 fresh thyme sprig

pepper

1 Make a demi-glace sauce. Mix the beef stock and Espagnole sauce together in a saucepan and warm over a low heat for 10 minutes, stirring occasionally.

2 Meanwhile, place the red wine, red wine vinegar, shallots, bay leaf and thyme in a saucepan, bring to the boil over a medium heat and cook until the sauce is reduced by three-quarters.

3 Strain the demi-glace sauce and add to the pan containing the red wine sauce and simmer for about 20 minutes, stirring occasionally. Season with pepper to taste and strain the sauce before using.

How to Use This Book

Each recipe contains a wealth of useful information, including a breakdown

of nutritional quantities, preparation and cooking times, and level of difficulty.

All of this information is explained in detail below.

The ingredients for each recipe are listed in the order that they are used.

The nutritional information provided for each recipe is per serving or per portion. Optional ingredients, variations or serving suggestions have not been included in the calculations.

A full-colour photograph of the finished dish.

The method is clearly explained with step-by-step instructions that are easy to follow.

Cook's tips provide useful information regarding ingredients or cooking techniques.

The number of stars represents the difficulty of each recipe, ranging from very easy (1 star) to challenging (4 stars).

This amount of time represents the preparation of ingredients, including cooling, chilling and soaking times.

This represents the cooking time.

Soups

A tasty soup or starter that complements the dishes to follow can help set the tone for the rest of a meal, and the wide variety of dishes in this section offer a host of options to match almost any main course. The soups can also be light meals in themselves, served with bread.

One of the great strengths of soups is their versatility. Although the best results are obtained from using fresh ingredients, soups are still a quick and easy way of using up leftovers. Soup recipes can also be stretched to serve more people simply by increasing the amount of stock used and can be thickened by adding more vegetables. If you have the time, making your own stock is a healthy alternative to using granules or stock cubes, which can contain salt and flavourings. They may also have too strong a taste.

This soup is best made with white onions, which have a much milder flavour than the more usual brown variety. If these are unavailable, use the large Spanish onions instead.

Tuscan Onion Soup

SERVES 4

50 g/1¾ oz pancetta, diced
1 tbsp olive oil
4 large white onions, sliced thinly in rings
3 garlic cloves, chopped
850 ml/1½ pints hot chicken or ham stock
4 slices ciabatta or other Italian bread
50 g/1¾ oz butter
75 g/2¾ oz Gruyère or Cheddar cheese, grated coarsely
salt and pepper

1 Dry fry the pancetta in a large saucepan over a medium-low heat for about 3–4 minutes, or until it starts to brown. Remove the pancetta from the saucepan and reserve until required.

2 Add the olive oil to the saucepan, add the onions and garlic and cook over a high heat for 4 minutes. Reduce the heat, cover and cook for 15 minutes, or until they are lightly caramelised.

3 Add the stock to the saucepan and bring to the boil over a medium heat. Reduce the heat and simmer, covered, for about 10 minutes.

4 Toast the slices of ciabatta on both sides, under a preheated hot grill, for 2–3 minutes, or until golden. Spread the ciabatta with the butter and top with the Gruyère or Cheddar cheese. Cut the bread into bite-sized pieces.

5 Add the pancetta to the soup and season to taste with salt and pepper. Ladle the soup into 4 serving bowls and top with the toasted bread. Serve.

NUTRITION
Calories 390; Sugars 0 g; Protein 9g;
Carbohydrate 15 g; Fat 33 g; Saturates 14 g

 very easy

 5–10 mins

40–45 mins

🍳 **COOK'S TIP**

Pancetta is similar to bacon, but it is air- and salt-cured for about 6 months. It is available from most delicatessens and some large supermarkets. If you cannot obtain pancetta, use unsmoked bacon instead.

This wonderful combination of cannellini beans, vegetables and vermicelli is made even richer by the addition of pesto, dried mushrooms and Parmesan cheese.

Vegetable *and* Bean Soup

1 Slice the aubergine into rings about 1-cm/½-inch thick, then cut each ring into 4 pieces.

2 Cut the tomatoes and potato into small dice. Cut the carrot into sticks, about 2.5-cm/1-inch long and cut the leek into rings.

3 Place the cannellini beans and their liquid in a large saucepan. Add the aubergine, tomatoes, potatoes, carrot and leek, stirring to mix.

4 Add the stock to the saucepan and bring to the boil over a medium heat. Reduce the heat and simmer for 15 minutes.

5 Add the basil, dried mushrooms and their soaking liquid and the vermicelli and simmer for 5 minutes, or until all the vegetables are tender. Remove the pan from the heat and stir in the pesto.

6 Ladle the soup into 4 warmed serving bowls and serve immediately with freshly grated Parmesan cheese, if you wish.

SERVES 4

1 small aubergine
2 large tomatoes
1 potato, peeled
1 carrot
1 leek
425 g/15 oz canned cannellini beans
850 ml/1½ pints hot vegetable or
    chicken stock
2 tsp dried basil
15 g/½ oz dried porcini mushrooms, soaked
    for 20 minutes in enough warm water
    to cover
50 g/1 ¾ oz dried vermicelli
3 tbsp pesto (shop bought)
freshly grated Parmesan cheese, to
    serve (optional)

NUTRITION
Calories *294*; Sugars *2 g*; Protein *11 g*;
Carbohydrate *30 g*; Fat *16 g*; Saturates *2 g*

⭐⭐   easy

          30 mins

          30 mins

A thick vegetable soup, which is a delicious meal in itself. Serve with Parmesan cheese and lots of warm sun-dried tomato bread.

Chick-pea Soup

SERVES 4

2 tbsp olive oil
2 leeks, sliced
2 courgettes, diced
2 garlic cloves, crushed
800 g/1 lb 2 oz canned chopped tomatoes
1 tbsp tomato purée
1 bay leaf
850 ml/1½ pints chicken stock
400 g/14 oz canned chick-peas, drained and rinsed
225 g/8 oz fresh spinach
salt and pepper

to serve
freshly grated Parmesan cheese
sun-dried tomato bread

1 Heat the olive oil in a large saucepan over a medium heat. Add the leeks and courgettes and cook briskly for 5 minutes, stirring constantly.

2 Add the garlic, chopped tomatoes, tomato purée, bay leaf, chicken stock and the chick-peas.

3 Bring to the boil and simmer for 5 minutes.

4 Shred the spinach finely, add to the soup and cook for 2 minutes. Season to taste with salt and pepper.

5 Remove the bay leaf and discard. Ladle the soup into 4 warmed serving bowls and serve immediately with freshly grated Parmesan cheese and warm sun-dried tomato bread.

NUTRITION
Calories *297*; Sugars *0 g*; Protein *11 g*;
Carbohydrate *24 g*; Fat *18 g*; Saturates *2 g*

very easy

5 mins

15 mins

👨‍🍳 **COOK'S TIP**

Chick-peas are used extensively in North African cuisine and are also found in Spanish, Middle Eastern and Indian cooking. They have a nutty flavour with a firm texture and are excellent canned.

The Calabrian mountains in southern Italy provide large amounts of wild mushrooms. They are rich in flavour and colour and make a wonderful soup.

Calabrian Mushroom Soup

1 Heat the olive oil in a large frying pan over a low heat. Add the onion and fry for 3–4 minutes, or until soft and golden.

2 Wipe each mushroom with a damp cloth and cut any large mushrooms into smaller bite-sized pieces.

3 Add the mushrooms to the pan, stirring quickly to coat them well in the oil.

4 Add the milk to the pan, bring to the boil over a medium heat, cover and simmer for about 5 minutes. Gradually stir in the hot vegetable stock.

5 Toast the bread on both sides, under a preheated hot grill, for 2–3 minutes, or until golden.

6 Mix the butter and garlic together, then spoon generously over the toast.

7 Place the toast in the base of a large tureen or divide it among 4 warmed serving bowls and pour over the hot soup. Top with the grated Gruyère cheese and serve immediately.

SERVES 4

2 tbsp olive oil
1 onion, chopped
450g/1 lb mixed mushrooms, such as ceps, oyster and button
300 ml/10 fl oz milk
850 ml/1½ pints hot vegetable stock
8 slices of rustic bread or French stick
50 g/1¾ oz butter, melted
2 garlic cloves, crushed
75 g/2¾ oz finely grated Gruyère cheese
salt and pepper

NUTRITION
Calories *452*; Sugars *5 g*; Protein *15 g*; Carbohydrate *42 g*; Fat *26 g*; Saturates *12 g*

 easy
5 mins
25–30 mins

COOK'S TIP

Mushrooms absorb liquid, which can lessen the flavour and affect cooking properties. Wipe them with a damp cloth rather than rinsing them in water.

Plum tomatoes are ideal for making soups and sauces, as they have denser, less watery flesh than round varieties.

Tomato *and* Pasta Soup

SERVES 4

55 g/2 oz unsalted butter
1 large onion, chopped
600 ml/1 pint vegetable stock
900 g/2 lb Italian plum tomatoes, peeled
    and roughly chopped
pinch of bicarbonate of soda
225 g/8 oz dried fusilli
1 tbsp caster sugar
150 ml/5 fl oz double cream
salt and pepper
fresh basil leaves, to garnish
deep-fried croûtons, to serve

1 Melt the butter in a large saucepan over a low heat. Add the onion and fry for 3 minutes. Add 300 ml/10 fl oz of vegetable stock to the pan, with the chopped tomatoes and bicarbonate of soda. Bring the soup to the boil, then simmer for 20 minutes.

2 Remove the pan from the heat and leave to cool. Transfer the soup to a blender or food processor and process until a purée forms. Pour through a fine sieve back into the rinsed out saucepan.

3 Add the remaining vegetable stock and the pasta to the saucepan, and season to taste with salt and pepper.

4 Add the sugar to the saucepan, bring to the boil over a medium heat, then reduce the heat and simmer for about 15 minutes.

5 Pour the soup into 4 large, warmed serving bowls, swirl the cream on the top of the soup and garnish with fresh basil leaves. Serve immediately with deep-fried croûtons.

NUTRITION
Calories *503*; Sugars *16 g*; Protein 9 *g*;
Carbohydrate *59 g*; Fat *28 g*; Saturates *17 g*

easy

5 mins

50–55 mins

🍳 **COOK'S TIP**

To make orange and tomato soup, simply use half the quantity of vegetable stock, topped up with the same amount of fresh orange juice, and garnish the soup with orange rind.

This is a hearty and filling soup, as it contains rice and tender strips of lamb. Serve before a light main course.

Lamb *and* Rice Soup

1 Using a sharp knife, trim any fat from the lamb and cut the meat into thin strips. Reserve until required.

2 Bring a large saucepan of lightly salted water to the boil over a medium heat. Add the rice, bring back to the boil, stir once, then reduce the heat and cook for 10–15 minutes, or until tender.

3 Drain the rice thoroughly, then rinse under cold running water, drain again and reserve until required.

4 Meanwhile, place the lamb stock in a large saucepan and bring to the boil over a medium heat.

5 Add the lamb strips, leek, garlic, soy sauce and rice wine vinegar to the stock in the pan. Reduce the heat, cover and simmer for 10 minutes, or until the lamb is tender and cooked through.

6 Add the mushroom slices and the rice to the saucepan and cook for a further 2–3 minutes, or until the mushroom is completely cooked through. Ladle the soup into 4 warmed serving bowls and serve immediately.

SERVES 4

150 g/5½ oz lean lamb
50 g/1¾ oz rice
850 ml/1½ pints lamb stock
1 leek, sliced
1 garlic clove, sliced thinly
2 tsp light soy sauce
1 tsp rice wine vinegar
1 medium open-cap mushroom, sliced thinly
salt

NUTRITION
Calories *116*; Sugars *0.2 g*; Protein *9 g*; Carbohydrate *12 g*; Fat *4 g*; Saturates *2 g*

⊛⊛ easy
◔ 5 mins
◷ 35 mins

 COOK'S TIP

Use a few dried Chinese mushrooms, rehydrated according to the packet instructions and chopped, as an alternative to the open-cap mushroom. Add the Chinese mushrooms with the lamb in step 4.

Chinese mushrooms add an intense flavour to this soup, which is unique. Try to obtain them if you can, otherwise use open-cap mushrooms, sliced.

Chilli Fish Soup

SERVES 4

15 g/¹⁄₂ oz dried Chinese mushrooms
2 tbsp sunflower oil
1 onion, sliced
100 g/3¹⁄₂ oz mangetout
100 g/3¹⁄₂ oz bamboo shoots, drained
3 tbsp sweet chilli sauce
1.2 litres/2 pints fish or vegetable stock
3 tbsp light soy sauce
2 tbsp fresh coriander, plus extra
　to garnish (optional)
450 g/1 lb cod fillet, skinned and cubed

1 Place the mushrooms in a large bowl and pour over enough almost boiling water to cover. Leave to stand for 5 minutes, then drain the mushrooms thoroughly. Using a sharp knife, roughly chop the mushrooms.

2 Heat the sunflower oil in a preheated wok over a medium heat. Add the onion and stir-fry for 5 minutes, or until softened.

3 Add the mangetout, bamboo shoots, chilli sauce, stock and soy sauce and bring to the boil over a medium heat.

4 Reduce the heat, add the coriander and cubed fish, then simmer for about 5 minutes, or until the fish is cooked through.

5 Ladle the soup into 4 warmed serving bowls, garnish with extra coriander, if you wish, and serve immediately.

NUTRITION
Calories *238*; Sugars *1.4 g*; Protein *21.4 g*;
Carbohydrate *3.2 g*; Fat *7.2 g*; Saturates *1 g*

easy
10 mins
20 mins

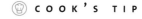 **COOK'S TIP**

There are many different varieties of dried mushrooms, but shiitake are best in this recipe. They are not cheap, but a small amount will go a long way.

Two classic ingredients in Chinese cooking, ginger and soy sauce, are blended together in this recipe for a very special soup. Light soy sauce is used as it will not overpower all the other flavours.

Chinese Crab Soup *with* Ginger

1 Place the carrot, leek, bay leaf and fish stock in a large saucepan and bring to the boil over a medium heat. Reduce the heat, cover and simmer for about 10 minutes, or until the vegetables are nearly tender.

2 Meanwhile, remove the meat from the cooked crabs. Break off the claws, break the joints and remove the meat (you may require a fork or skewer for this). Add the crabmeat to the stock in the saucepan.

3 Add the ginger, soy sauce and star anise to the fish stock and bring to the boil over a medium heat. Reduce the heat and simmer for about 10 minutes, or until the vegetables are tender and the crab is heated through. Season to taste with salt and pepper.

4 Ladle the soup into 4 warmed serving bowls and serve immediately.

SERVES 4

1 carrot, chopped
1 leek, chopped
1 bay leaf
850 ml/1½ pints fish stock
2 medium-sized cooked crabs
2.5-cm/1-inch piece fresh root ginger, grated
1 tsp light soy sauce
½ tsp ground star anise
salt and pepper

NUTRITION
Calories *145*; Sugars *2.4 g*; Protein *40 g*; Carbohydrate *2.7 g*; Fat *5.7 g*; Saturates *2.6 g*

⭐⭐ easy
🕐 15 mins
🕐 25 mins

COOK'S TIP

If fresh crabmeat is unavailable, use drained canned crabmeat or thawed frozen crabmeat instead.

Tender cooked chicken strips and baby sweetcorn are the main flavours in this delicious clear soup, with just a hint of ginger.

Curried Chicken Soup

SERVES 4

175 g/6 oz canned sweetcorn, drained
850 ml/1½ pints chicken stock
350 g/12 oz cooked, lean chicken, cut into strips
16 baby sweetcorn
1 tsp Chinese curry powder
1-cm/½-inch piece fresh root ginger, grated
3 tbsp light soy sauce
2 tbsp snipped fresh chives

1 Place the canned sweetcorn in a food processor, with 150 ml/5 fl oz of the chicken stock and process until a smooth purée forms.

2 Rub the sweetcorn purée through a fine sieve, pressing gently with the back of a spoon to separate the husks from the corn.

3 Pour the remaining chicken stock into a large saucepan and add the strips of cooked chicken. Stir in the sweetcorn purée and mix well.

4 Add the baby sweetcorn and bring the soup to the boil over a medium heat. Cook for 10 minutes.

5 Add the Chinese curry powder, grated ginger and soy sauce and stir thoroughly. Cook the soup for a further 10–15 minutes.

6 Stir in the snipped chives, then ladle the soup into 4 warmed serving bowls. Serve immediately.

NUTRITION
Calories *206*; Sugars *5 g*; Protein *29 g*;
Carbohydrate *13 g*; Fat *5 g*; Saturates *1 g*

easy

5 mins

30 mins

🧑‍🍳 **COOK'S TIP**

Prepare the soup up to 24 hours in advance without adding the chicken. Leave to cool, cover and store in the refrigerator. Add the chicken and heat the soup through thoroughly before serving.

This satisfying soup makes a good lunch or supper dish and you can use any vegetables that you have at hand. Children will love the tiny pasta shapes.

Chicken *and* Pasta Soup

1 Using a sharp knife, remove any skin from the chicken breasts and discard, then finely dice the chicken.

2 Heat the sunflower oil in a large saucepan over a medium heat. Add the chicken, onion, carrots and cauliflower and quickly sauté until they are lightly coloured.

3 Stir in the stock and herbs. Bring to the boil and add the pasta shapes. Return to the boil, cover and simmer for 10 minutes, stirring occasionally to prevent the pasta sticking together.

4 Season to taste with salt and pepper. Ladle the soup into 4 warmed serving bowls and sprinkle with the Parmesan cheese (if using). Serve immediately with fresh crusty bread.

S E R V E S   4

350 g/12 oz boneless chicken breasts
2 tbsp sunflower oil
1 medium onion, diced
250 g/9 oz carrots, diced
250 g/9 oz cauliflower florets
850 ml/1½ pints chicken stock
2 tsp dried mixed herbs
125 g/4½ oz small dried pasta shapes
salt and pepper
freshly grated Parmesan cheese,
    for sprinkling (optional)
crusty bread, to serve

N U T R I T I O N
Calories *185*; Sugars *5 g*; Protein *17 g*;
Carbohydrate *20 g*; Fat *5 g*; Saturates *1 g*

⭐⭐	easy
🕐	5 mins
🕐	15–20 mins

 C O O K ' S   T I P

You can use any small pasta shapes for this soup – try conchigliette, ditalini, or even spaghetti broken up into small pieces. To make a fun soup for children, try adding animal-shaped or alphabet pasta.

This satisfying soup can be served as a main course. You can add a mixture of rice and sweet peppers to make it even more hearty, as well as colourful.

Chicken *and* Leek Soup

SERVES 4

25 g/1 oz butter
350 g/12 oz skinless, boneless chicken, cut into 2.5-cm/ 1-inch pieces
350 g/12 oz leeks, cut into 2.5-cm/ 1-inch pieces
1.2 litres/2 pints chicken stock
1 bouquet garni sachet
8 stoned prunes
salt and white pepper

1 Melt the butter in a large, heavy-based saucepan over a medium heat. Add the chicken and leeks and fry for 8 minutes, stirring occasionally.

2 Add the chicken stock and bouquet garni sachet to the pan and stir well. Season to taste with salt and pepper.

3 Bring the soup to the boil over a medium heat, then reduce the heat and simmer for 45 minutes.

4 Add the prunes to the saucepan and simmer for about 20 minutes.

5 Remove the bouquet garni sachet from the soup and discard. Ladle the soup into 4 warmed serving bowls and serve.

NUTRITION
Calories *183*; Sugars *4 g*; Protein *21 g*; Carbohydrate *4 g*; Fat *9 g*; Saturates *5 g*

 very easy

 5 mins

1 hr 15 mins

 **COOK'S TIP**

Instead of the bouquet garni sachet, you can use a bunch of fresh mixed herbs, tied together with string. Choose herbs such as parsley, thyme and rosemary.

Smoked haddock gives this soup a wonderfully rich flavour, while the mashed potatoes and cream thicken and enrich the stock.

Smoked Haddock Soup

1 Place the fish, onion, garlic and water in a large, heavy-based saucepan, then bring to the boil over a medium heat. Reduce the heat, cover and simmer for 15–20 minutes.

2 Remove the fish from the saucepan. Strip off the skin and remove all the bones and reserve both. Flake the flesh finely with a fork.

3 Return the skin and bones to the cooking liquid and simmer for 10 minutes. Strain, discarding the skin and bones, then pour the cooking liquid into a clean saucepan.

4 Add the milk and flaked fish to the saucepan and season to taste with salt and pepper. Bring to the boil over a medium heat, then reduce the heat and simmer for about 3 minutes.

5 Gradually whisk in sufficient mashed potato to give a fairly thick soup, then stir in the butter and sharpen to taste with lemon juice.

6 Add the fromage frais and 3 tablespoons of the chopped parsley. Reheat gently and adjust the seasoning, if necessary. Ladle the soup into 4 warmed serving bowls, sprinkle with the remaining parsley and serve immediately.

SERVES 4

225 g/8 oz smoked haddock fillet
1 onion, chopped finely
1 garlic clove, crushed
600 ml/1 pint water
600 ml/1 pint skimmed milk
225–350 g/8–12 oz hot mashed potatoes
2 tbsp butter
about 1 tbsp lemon juice
6 tbsp low-fat natural fromage frais
4 tbsp chopped fresh parsley
salt and pepper

NUTRITION
Calories *169*; Sugars *8 g*; Protein *16 g*;
Carbohydrate *16 g*; Fat *5 g*; Saturates *3 g*

easy

25 mins

40 mins

A mouthwatering, healthy, vegetable, bean and bacon soup. Serve with plenty of fresh granary or crusty wholemeal bread.

Bacon, Bean *and* Garlic Soup

SERVES 4

225 g/8 oz lean smoked back bacon rashers
1 carrot, sliced thinly
1 celery stick, sliced thinly
1 onion, chopped
1 tbsp oil
3 garlic cloves, sliced
700 ml/1¼ pints hot vegetable stock
200 g/7 oz canned chopped tomatoes
1 tbsp chopped fresh thyme
400 g/14 oz canned cannellini beans, drained and rinsed
1 tbsp tomato purée
salt and pepper
freshly grated Cheddar cheese, to garnish

1 Chop 2 slices of the bacon and place in a bowl. Cook in the microwave on High power for 3–4 minutes, until the fat runs out and the bacon is well cooked. Stir the bacon halfway through cooking to separate the pieces. Transfer the bacon to a plate lined with kitchen paper and leave to cool. When cool, the bacon pieces should be crisp and dry.

2 Place the carrot, celery, onion and oil in a large bowl. Cover and cook on High power for 4 minutes.

3 Chop the remaining bacon and add to the bowl with the garlic. Cover and cook on High power for 2 minutes.

4 Add the stock, the chopped tomatoes, thyme, cannellini beans and tomato purée. Cover and cook on High power for 8 minutes, stirring halfway through. Season to taste with salt and pepper. Ladle the soup into 4 warmed serving bowls and sprinkle with the crisp bacon and grated Cheddar cheese. Serve immediately.

NUTRITION
Calories *261*; Sugars *5 g*; Protein *32 g*; Carbohydrate *25 g*; Fat *8 g*; Saturates *2 g*

easy
5 mins
20 mins

 COOK'S TIP

For a more substantial soup add 55 g/2 oz small dried pasta shapes or short lengths of spaghetti with the stock and tomatoes. You will also need to add an extra 150 ml/5 fl oz vegetable stock.

This nutritious soup uses split red lentils and carrots as its two main ingredients, and includes a selection of spices to give it an extra kick.

Spicy Dhal *and* Carrot Soup

1 Place the lentils in a large, heavy-based saucepan with 850 ml/1½ pints of the vegetable stock, the carrots, onions, tomatoes and garlic. Bring the mixture to the boil over a medium heat, then reduce the heat, cover and simmer for 30 minutes, or until the vegetables and lentils are tender.

2 Meanwhile, heat the ghee in a small saucepan over a low heat. Add the ground cumin, coriander, chilli and turmeric and fry for 1 minute. Remove from the heat and stir in the lemon juice. Season with salt to taste.

3 Working in batches, transfer the soup to a food processor or blender and process until smooth. Return the soup to the saucepan, add the spice mixture and the remaining 300 ml/10 fl oz of the stock and cook over a low heat for 10 minutes.

4 Add the milk and taste and adjust the seasoning, if necessary. Stir in the chopped coriander and reheat gently. Ladle the soup into 4 warmed serving bowls and serve hot with a swirl of yogurt.

SERVES 4

125 g/4½ oz split red lentils, rinsed and drained
1.2 litres/2 pints vegetable stock
350 g/12 oz carrots, sliced
2 onions, chopped
225 g/8 oz canned chopped tomatoes
2 garlic cloves, chopped
2 tbsp ghee or vegetable oil
1 tsp ground cumin
1 tsp ground coriander
1 fresh green chilli, deseeded and chopped
½ tsp ground turmeric
1 tbsp lemon juice
300 ml/10 fl oz milk
2 tbsp chopped fresh coriander
salt
natural yogurt, to serve

NUTRITION
Calories *173*; Sugars *11 g*; Protein *9 g*;
Carbohydrate *24 g*; Fat *5 g*; Saturates *1 g*

  very easy
  15 mins
  45 mins

For a warming, satisfying meal on a cold day, this lentil soup is packed full of flavour and goodness.

Spicy Lentil Soup

SERVES 4

115 g/4 oz split red lentils
2 tsp vegetable oil
1 large onion, chopped finely
2 garlic cloves, crushed
1 tsp ground cumin
1 tsp ground coriander
1 tsp garam masala
2 tbsp tomato purée
1 litre/1¾ pints vegetable stock
350 g/12 oz canned sweetcorn, drained
salt and pepper

to serve
low-fat natural yogurt
chopped fresh parsley
warm pitta bread

1 Place the split red lentils in a sieve and rinse thoroughly under cold running water. Drain thoroughly and reserve until required.

2 Heat the vegetable oil in a large non-stick frying pan over a medium heat. Add the onion and garlic and fry gently until softened, but not browned.

3 Stir in the cumin, coriander, garam masala, tomato purée and 4 tablespoons of the vegetable stock. Mix well and simmer gently for 2 minutes.

4 Add the lentils to the pan, then pour in the remaining stock. Bring to the boil over a medium heat, then reduce the heat, cover and simmer for 1 hour, or until the lentils are tender and the soup thickened. Stir in the sweetcorn and heat through for 5 minutes. Season to taste with salt and pepper.

5 Ladle the soup into 4 warmed serving bowls and top each with a spoonful of yogurt and a sprinkling of parsley. Serve immediately with pitta bread.

NUTRITION

Calories *155*; Sugars *4 g*; Protein *11 g*;
Carbohydrate *22 g*; Fat *3 g*; Saturates *0.4 g*

 easy

1 hr

1 hr 15 mins

🍳 COOK'S TIP

Many of the ready-prepared ethnic breads available today either contain fat or are brushed with oil before baking. Always check the ingredients list for the fat content before buying.

This is a real winter warmer – pieces of tender beef and chunky mixed vegetables are cooked in a stock flavoured with sherry.

Chunky Potato *and* Beef Soup

1 Heat the vegetable oil in a large saucepan over a medium heat. Add the strips of steak and cook for 3 minutes, turning constantly.

2 Add the potatoes, carrot, celery and leeks. Cook, stirring constantly, for a further 5 minutes.

3 Pour in the beef stock and bring to the boil over a medium heat. Reduce the heat until the liquid is simmering gently. Add the sliced baby sweetcorn and the bouquet garni.

4 Cook the soup for a further 20 minutes, or until the meat and the vegetables are tender.

5 Remove the bouquet garni from the saucepan and discard. Stir the dry sherry into the soup, then season to taste with salt and pepper.

6 Ladle the soup into 4 warmed serving bowls and garnish with chopped fresh parsley. Serve immediately with crusty bread.

SERVES 4

2 tbsp vegetable oil
225 g/8 oz lean braising or frying steak, cut into strips
225 g/8 oz new potatoes, halved
1 carrot, diced
2 celery sticks, sliced
2 leeks, sliced
850 ml/1½ pints beef stock
8 baby sweetcorn, sliced
1 bouquet garni
2 tbsp dry sherry
salt and pepper
chopped fresh parsley, to garnish
crusty bread, to serve

NUTRITION
Calories *187*; Sugars *3 g*; Protein *14 g*;
Carbohydrate *12 g*; Fat *9 g*; Saturates *2 g*

⭐⭐ easy
🕐 5 mins
🕐 35 mins

COOK'S TIP

Make double quantity of soup and freeze the remainder in a rigid container for later use. When ready to use, leave in the refrigerator to thaw thoroughly, then heat until piping hot.

Thai soups are very quickly and easily put together, and are cooked so that each ingredient can still be tasted in the finished dish.

Mushroom *and* Ginger Soup

SERVES 4

15 g/½ oz dried Chinese mushrooms or
   125 g/4½ oz field or chestnut mushrooms
1 litre/1¾ pints hot vegetable stock
125 g/4½ oz thread egg noodles
2 tsp sunflower oil
3 garlic cloves, crushed
2.5-cm/1-inch piece fresh root ginger,
   shredded finely
½ tsp mushroom ketchup
1 tsp light soy sauce
125 g/4½ oz bean sprouts
fresh coriander leaves, to garnish

1 Soak the dried Chinese mushrooms (if using) for at least 30 minutes in 300 ml/10 fl oz of the hot vegetable stock. Remove and discard the stalks from the fresh mushrooms, then slice. Drain the dried mushrooms and reserve the stock.

2 Bring a large saucepan of water to the boil over a medium heat. Add the noodles and cook for 2–3 minutes. Drain and rinse, then reserve.

3 Heat the sunflower oil in a preheated wok or large, heavy-based frying pan over a high heat. Add the garlic and ginger. Stir and add all the mushrooms and stir-fry for 2 minutes.

4 Add the remaining vegetable stock with the reserved stock and bring to the boil over a medium heat. Add the mushroom ketchup and soy sauce.

5 Stir in the bean sprouts and cook for 1 minute. Put some noodles into 4 serving bowls and ladle the soup on top. Garnish with a few coriander leaves and serve immediately.

NUTRITION
Calories *74*; Sugars *1 g*; Protein *3 g*;
Carbohydrate *9 g*; Fat *3 g*; Saturates *0.4 g*

easy

1 hr 30 mins

15 mins

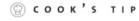 **COOK'S TIP**

Rice noodles contain no fat and are ideal for for anyone on a low-fat diet.

Whole young spinach leaves add vibrant colour to this unusual soup. Serve with hot, crusty bread for a nutritious light meal.

Yogurt *and* Spinach Soup

1 Pour the chicken stock into a large saucepan. Season to taste with salt and pepper and bring to the boil over a medium heat. Add the rice and simmer for 10 minutes until barely cooked. Remove the saucepan from the heat.

2 Mix the water and cornflour together to a smooth paste. Pour the yogurt into a second saucepan and stir in the cornflour mixture. Set the saucepan over a low heat and bring the yogurt to the boil, stirring with a wooden spoon in one direction only. This will stabilise the yogurt and prevent it curdling on contact with the hot stock. When the yogurt has reached boiling point, stand the saucepan on a heat diffuser and simmer for 10 minutes, then remove the heat and cool slightly before stirring in the egg yolks.

3 Pour the yogurt mixture into the stock, stir in the lemon juice and stir to blend thoroughly. Keep the soup warm, but do not allow it to boil.

4 Blanch the washed and drained spinach leaves in a large saucepan of boiling, salted water for 2–3 minutes, or until just softened but not wilted. Tip the spinach into a colander, drain well and stir into the soup. Warm through. Taste the soup and adjust the seasoning, if necessary. Ladle the soup into wide, shallow soup plates and serve immediately.

SERVES 4

600 ml/1 pint chicken stock
4 tbsp long-grain rice, rinsed and drained
4 tbsp water
1 tbsp cornflour
600 ml/1 pint low-fat natural yogurt
3 egg yolks, beaten lightly
juice of 1 lemon
350 g/12 oz young spinach leaves, washed
   and drained
salt and pepper

NUTRITION
Calories 227; Sugars 13 g; Protein 14 g;
Carbohydrate 29 g; Fat 7 g; Saturates 2 g

moderate

15 mins

30 mins

This hearty soup uses a variety of green vegetables with a subtle flavouring of ground coriander. A finishing touch of thinly sliced leeks adds texture.

Gardener's Broth

SERVES 4

40 g/1½ oz butter
1 onion, chopped
1–2 garlic cloves, crushed
1 large leek
225 g/8 oz Brussels sprouts
125 g/4½ oz French or runner beans
1.2 litres/2 pints vegetable stock
125 g/4½ oz frozen peas
1 tbsp lemon juice
½ tsp ground coriander
4 tbsp double cream
salt and pepper

melba toast
4–6 slices white bread

NUTRITION

Calories *169*; Sugars *5 g*; Protein *4 g*;
Carbohydrate *8 g*; Fat *13 g*; Saturates *5 g*

moderate

10 mins

45 mins

1 Melt the butter in a saucepan over a low heat. Add the onion and garlic and fry, stirring occasionally, until they start to soften, but not colour.

2 Slice the white part of the leek very thinly and reserve. Slice the remaining leek, then slice the Brussels sprouts and thinly slice the beans.

3 Add the green part of the leeks, the Brussels sprouts and beans to the saucepan. Add the stock and bring to the boil over a medium heat, then reduce the heat and simmer for 10 minutes. Add the peas, seasoning, lemon juice and coriander. Cook for 10–15 minutes, or until the vegetables are tender.

4 Leave the soup to cool slightly, then transfer to a food processor or blender and process until smooth. Alternatively, rub through a sieve with the back of a spoon. Pour into a clean saucepan.

5 Add the reserved slices of leek to the soup, bring back to the boil and cook for 5 minutes, or until the leek is tender. Adjust the seasoning, stir in the cream and reheat gently.

6 To make the Melba toast, toast the bread on both sides under a preheated hot grill. Cut horizontally through the slices, then toast the uncooked sides until they curl up. Serve immediately with the soup.

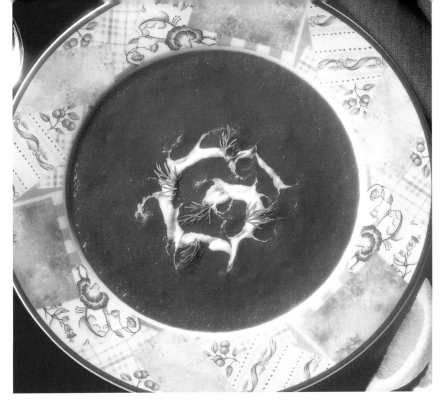

A deep red soup makes a stunning first course – and it's easy in the microwave. A swirl of soured cream gives a very pretty effect.

Beetroot *and* Potato Soup

1 Place the onion, potatoes, apple and water in a large bowl. Cover and cook in the microwave on High power for 10 minutes.

2 Stir in the cumin seeds and cook on High power for 1 minute.

3 Stir in the beetroot, bay leaf, thyme, lemon juice and vegetable stock. Cover and cook on High power for 12 minutes, stirring halfway through. Leave, uncovered, for 5 minutes.

4 Remove the bay leaf and discard. Strain the vegetables and reserve the liquid in a jug.

5 Place the vegetables with a little of the reserved liquid in a food processor or blender and process until a smooth and creamy purée forms. Alternatively, either mash the vegetable with a potato masher or rub through a sieve.

6 Pour the vegetable purée into a clean bowl with the reserved liquid and mix well. Season to taste with salt and pepper. Cover and cook on High power for 4–5 minutes, or until the soup is piping hot.

7 Ladle the soup into 6 warmed serving bowls. Swirl 1 tablespoon of soured cream into each serving and garnish with a few fresh dill sprigs.

SERVES 4

1 onion, chopped
350 g/12 oz potatoes, diced
1 small cooking apple, peeled, cored and grated
3 tbsp water
1 tsp cumin seeds
500 g/1 lb 2 oz cooked beetroot, peeled and diced
1 bay leaf
pinch of dried thyme
1 tsp lemon juice
600 ml/1 pint hot vegetable stock
4 tbsp soured cream
salt and pepper
fresh dill sprigs, to garnish

NUTRITION
Calories 120; Sugars 11 g; Protein 4 g; Carbohydrate 22 g; Fat 2 g; Saturates 1 g

easy

20 mins

30 mins

Snacks *and* Starters

All too frequently, leaf vegetables are overcooked and limp, with all the goodness and flavour boiled out, while salads are often nothing more than a dismal leaf or two of pale green lettuce with a slice of tomato and a dry ring of onion. Make the most of the wonderful range of fresh produce available in our shops and markets.

Steam broccoli and cabbage so they are colourful and crunchy. Enjoy the wonderfully appetising shades of orange and yellow peppers and the almost unbelievable purple-brown of aubergine. Try grating root vegetables – carrots and daikon or mooli – to add flavour and texture to garnishes and casseroles. Look out for red and curly lettuces to bring excitement to an enticing summer salad. Use sweet baby tomatoes in salads and on skewers, and raid your garden and windowsill for plenty of fresh mint sprigs and basil leaves.

Anyone who loves garlic will adore this dip – it is very potent! Serve it at a barbecue and dip raw vegetables or chunks of French bread into it.

Heavenly Garlic Dip

SERVES 4

2 garlic bulbs
6 tbsp olive oil
1 small onion, chopped finely
2 tbsp lemon juice
3 tbsp tahini
2 tbsp chopped fresh parsley
salt and pepper
1 fresh flat-leaf parsley sprig, to garnish

to serve
fresh vegetable crudités
French bread or warm pitta breads

1 Separate the garlic bulbs into individual cloves. Place them on a baking tray and roast in a preheated oven at 200°C/400°F/Gas Mark 6, for 8–10 minutes. Leave to cool for a few minutes.

2 When they are cool enough to handle, peel the garlic cloves, then chop them finely with a sharp knife.

3 Heat the olive oil in a saucepan or frying pan over a low heat. Add the garlic and onion and fry, stirring occasionally, for 8–10 minutes, or until softened. Remove the pan from the heat.

4 Mix in the lemon juice, tahini and parsley. Season to taste with salt and pepper. Transfer the dip to a small heatproof bowl and keep warm while you prepare the vegetable crudités.

5 When ready to serve, garnish the dip with a parsley sprig and serve with the vegetable crudités, chunks of French bread or warm pitta breads.

NUTRITION
Calories *344*; Sugars *2 g*; Protein *6 g*;
Carbohydrate *3 g*; Fat *34 g*; Saturates *5 g*

 very easy

15 mins

20 mins

COOK'S TIP

If you come across smoked garlic, use it in this recipe – it tastes wonderful. There is no need to roast the smoked garlic, so omit the first step. This dip can also be used to baste vegetarian burgers.

This wonderful soft cheese pâté is fragrant with the aroma of fresh herbs and garlic. Serve with triangles of Melba toast for a perfect starter.

Cheese, Garlic *and* Herb Pâté

1 Melt the butter in a small frying pan over a low heat. Add the garlic and spring onions and fry for 3–4 minutes, or until softened. Leave to cool.

2 Beat the soft cheese in a large mixing bowl until smooth, then add the garlic and spring onions. Stir in the chopped mixed herbs and mix well.

3 Add the Cheddar cheese, season to taste with salt and pepper and work the mixture together to form a stiff paste. Cover and chill in the refrigerator until ready to serve.

4 Toast the slices of bread on both sides, then cut off the crusts. Using a sharp bread knife, cut through the slices horizontally to make very thin slices. Cut into triangles, then lightly grill the untoasted sides under a preheated hot grill until golden.

5 Arrange the mixed salad leaves on 4 serving plates with the cherry tomatoes. Pile the cheese pâté on top and sprinkle with a little paprika. Garnish with fresh flat-leaf parsley sprigs and serve with the toast.

SERVES 4

15 g/½ oz butter
1 garlic clove, crushed
3 spring onions, chopped finely
125 g/4½ oz full-fat soft cheese
2 tbsp chopped fresh mixed herbs, such as parsley, chives, marjoram, oregano and basil
175 g/6 oz finely grated mature Cheddar cheese
4–6 slices of white bread from a medium-cut sliced loaf
salt and pepper

to garnish
ground paprika
4 fresh flat-leaf parsley sprigs

to serve
mixed salad leaves
cherry tomatoes

NUTRITION
Calories *392*; Sugars *1 g*; Protein *17 g*; Carbohydrate *18 g*; Fat *28 g*; Saturates *18 g*

⭐⭐ easy

 20 mins

 10 mins

This delicious smoked fish pâté is given a tart fruity flavour by the cooked gooseberries, which complement the fish perfectly.

Smoked Fish *and* Potato Pâté

SERVES 4

650 g/1 lb 7 oz floury potatoes, peeled and diced
300 g/10½ oz smoked mackerel, skinned and flaked
75 g/2¾ oz cooked gooseberries
2 tsp lemon juice
2 tbsp low-fat crème fraîche
1 tbsp capers, drained
1 gherkin, chopped
1 tbsp chopped pickled dill cucumber
1 tbsp chopped fresh dill
salt and pepper
lemon wedges, to garnish
warm crusty bread, to serve

1 Bring a saucepan of water to the boil over a medium heat. Add the potatoes and cook for 10 minutes, or until tender. Drain thoroughly.

2 Place the cooked potatoes in a food processor or blender. Add the smoked mackerel and process for 30 seconds, or until fairly smooth. Alternatively, place the ingredients in a large bowl and mash with a fork.

3 Add the gooseberries, lemon juice and crème fraîche to the fish and potato mixture. Blend for a further 10 seconds or mash well.

4 Stir in the capers, gherkin, dill cucumber and fresh dill. Season to taste with salt and pepper.

5 Transfer the fish pâté to a serving dish and garnish with lemon wedges. Serve with slices of warm crusty bread.

NUTRITION

Calories *418*; Sugars *4 g*; Protein *18 g*;
Carbohydrate *32 g*; Fat *25 g*; Saturates *6 g*

easy

20 mins

10 mins

COOK'S TIP

Use stewed, canned or bottled cooked gooseberries for convenience and to save time, or when fresh gooseberries are out of season.

Red split lentils are used in this spicy recipe for speed as they do not require presoaking. If you use other types of lentils, soak and precook them first according to the packet instructions.

Lentil Pâté

1 Heat the vegetable oil in a large saucepan over a medium heat. Add the onion and garlic and sauté for 2–3 minutes, stirring constantly. Add the spices and cook for a further 30 seconds. Stir in the vegetable stock and lentils and bring the mixture to the boil. Reduce the heat and simmer for 20 minutes, or until the lentils are cooked. Remove from the heat and drain off any excess moisture.

2 Transfer the mixture to a food processor and add the egg, milk, mango chutney and parsley. Blend until smooth.

3 Grease and line the base of a 450-g/ 1-lb loaf tin. Spoon the mixture into the tin and level the surface. Cover and cook in a preheated oven at 200°C/ 400°F/Gas Mark 6, for 40–45 minutes, or until firm.

4 Leave the pâté to cool in the tin for 20 minutes, then transfer to the refrigerator to cool completely. Turn out on to a serving plate, garnish with parsley sprigs and serve in slices with salad leaves and warm toast.

SERVES 4

1 tbsp vegetable oil, plus extra for greasing
1 onion, chopped
2 garlic cloves, crushed
1 tsp garam masala
½ tsp ground coriander
850 ml/1½ pints vegetable stock
175 g/6 oz red split lentils, washed
1 small egg
2 tbsp milk
2 tbsp mango chutney
2 tbsp chopped fresh parsley
fresh parsley sprigs, to garnish

to serve
salad leaves
warm toast

NUTRITION
Calories *267*; Sugars *12 g*; Protein *14 g*;
Carbohydrate *37 g*; Fat *8 g*; Saturates *1 g*

 easy

 25 mins

🕐 1 hr 15 mins

👩‍🍳 **COOK'S TIP**

Use other spices, such as chilli powder or Chinese five-spice powder, to flavour the pâté and add tomato relish or chilli relish instead of the mango chutney, if you prefer.

Cool, minty cucumber
and yogurt tzatziki and
garlicky black olive dips
taste superb with warm
pitta bread.

Tzatziki *and* Black Olive Dips

SERVES 4

½ cucumber
225 g/8 oz thick natural yogurt
1 tbsp chopped fresh mint
4 pitta breads
salt and pepper

black olive dip

2 garlic cloves, crushed
125 g/4½ oz stoned black olives
4 tbsp olive oil
2 tbsp lemon juice
1 tbsp chopped fresh parsley

to garnish

1 fresh mint sprig
1 fresh parsley sprig

1 To make the tzatziki, peel the cucumber and chop roughly. Sprinkle with salt and leave to stand for 15–20 minutes. Rinse under cold running water and drain thoroughly.

2 Mix the cucumber, yogurt and mint together. Season to taste with salt and pepper and transfer to a serving bowl. Cover and chill in the refrigerator for 20–30 minutes.

3 To make the black olive dip, put the crushed garlic and olives into a food processor or blender and process for 15–20 seconds. Alternatively, chop them very finely.

4 Add the olive oil, lemon juice and parsley to the food processor blender and process for a few more seconds. Alternatively, mix with the chopped garlic and olives and mash together. Season to taste with salt and pepper.

5 Wrap the pitta breads in tinfoil and either place over a hot barbecue for about 2–3 minutes, turning once to warm through, or heat in a preheated oven or under a preheated hot grill. Cut into pieces and serve with the tzatziki and black olive dips, garnished with mint and parsley sprigs.

NUTRITION

Calories *381*; Sugars *8 g*; Protein *11 g*;
Carbohydrate *52 g*; Fat *15 g*; Saturates *2 g*

⭐ very easy

🕐 1 hr

🕐 3 mins

🧑‍🍳 **COOK'S TIP**

Sprinkling the cucumber with salt draws out some of its moisture, making it crisper. If you are in a hurry, you can omit this procedure.

Hummus is especially good spread on these garlic toasts for a delicious starter or even as part of a light lunch.

Hummus Toasts *with* Olives

1 To make the hummus, firstly drain the chick-peas, reserving 2–3 tablespoons of the liquid. Place the chick-peas and half the reserved liquid in a food processor and blend, gradually adding the remaining liquid and lemon juice. Blend well after each addition until smooth.

2 Stir in the tahini and all but 1 teaspoon of the olive oil. Add the garlic, season to taste with salt and pepper and blend again until smooth.

3 Spoon the hummus into a serving dish. Drizzle the remaining olive oil over the top and leave to chill in the refrigerator while preparing the toasts.

4 To make the garlic toasts, lay the ciabatta slices on a grill rack in a layer.

5 Mix the garlic, coriander and olive oil together and drizzle over the bread. Cook under a preheated hot grill for 2–3 minutes, or until golden brown, turning once. To serve, garnish the hummus with chopped coriander and olives, then serve with the toasts.

SERVES 4

400 g/14 oz canned chick-peas
juice of 1 large lemon
6 tbsp tahini
2 tbsp olive oil
2 garlic cloves, crushed
salt and pepper

garlic toasts
1 ciabatta loaf, sliced
2 garlic cloves, crushed
1 tbsp chopped fresh coriander
4 tbsp olive oil

to garnish
1 tbsp chopped fresh coriander
6 stoned black olives, to garnish

NUTRITION
Calories *731*; Sugars *2 g*; Protein *22 g*;
Carbohydrate *39 g*; Fat *55 g*; Saturates *8 g*

⭐⭐⭐   moderate
     15 mins
     3 mins

Colourful marinated Mediterranean vegetables make a tasty starter. Serve with fresh bread or Tomato Toasts (see below).

Pepper Salad

SERVES 4

1 onion
2 red peppers
2 yellow peppers
3 tbsp olive oil
2 large courgettes, sliced
2 garlic cloves, sliced
1 tbsp balsamic vinegar
50 g/1¾ oz canned anchovy fillets, chopped
25 g/1 oz stoned black olives, halved
1 tbsp chopped fresh basil
salt and pepper
4 fresh basil sprigs, to garnish

tomato toasts

1 small stick of French bread
1 garlic clove, crushed
1 tomato, peeled and chopped
2 tbsp olive oil

1 Using a sharp knife, cut the onion into wedges. Deseed the peppers, then cut into thick slices.

2 Heat the olive oil in a large heavy-based frying pan over a low heat. Add the onion, peppers, courgettes and garlic and fry gently for about 20 minutes, stirring occasionally.

3 Add the vinegar, anchovies, olives and chopped basil. Season to taste with salt and pepper. Mix thoroughly and leave to cool.

4 To make the tomato toasts, cut the French bread diagonally into 1-cm/ ½-inch slices.

5 Mix the garlic, tomato and 1 tablespoon of olive oil together. Season to taste and spread thinly over each slice of bread.

6 Place the bread on a baking tray, drizzle with the remaining olive oil and bake in a preheated oven at 220°C/425°F/Gas Mark 7, for 5–10 minutes, or until crisp. Transfer the salad to 4 serving plates, garnish with basil sprigs and serve with the tomato toasts.

NUTRITION
Calories *234*; Sugars *4 g*; Protein *6 g*;
Carbohydrate *15 g*; Fat *17 g*; Saturates *2 g*

moderate

5–10 mins

35 mins

Using ripe tomatoes and the best extra virgin olive oil will make this Tuscan dish absolutely delicious.

Tuscan Ciabatta

1 Using a sharp knife, cut the cherry tomatoes in half.

2 Using a sharp knife, slice the sun-dried tomatoes into strips.

3 Place the cherry tomatoes and sun-dried tomatoes in a bowl. Add the olive oil and the basil leaves and, using a spoon, toss to mix. Season to taste with a little salt and pepper.

4 Toast the ciabatta slices on both sides under a preheated medium-hot grill. Using a sharp knife, cut the garlic cloves in half.

5 Rub the garlic, cut-side down, over both sides of the toasted ciabatta bread.

6 Put the ciabatta bread on to a large serving plate or 4 warmed plates and top with the tomato mixture. Serve immediately.

SERVES 4

300 g/10½ oz cherry tomatoes
4 sun-dried tomatoes
4 tbsp extra virgin olive oil
16 fresh basil leaves, shredded
8 slices ciabatta
2 garlic cloves
salt and pepper

NUTRITION
Calories *308*; Sugars *3 g*; Protein *7 g*;
Carbohydrate *37 g*; Fat *15 g*; Saturates *2 g*

⭐⭐⭐ moderate
🕐 10 mins
🕐 5 mins

 COOK'S TIP

Ciabatta is an Italian rustic bread, which is slightly holey and quite chewy. It is excellent in this recipe as it absorbs the full flavour of the garlic and extra virgin olive oil.

This colourful fresh salad is delicious at any time of the year. Prosciutto di Parma is thought to be the best ham in the world.

Figs *and* Parma Ham

SERVES 4

40 g/1½ oz rocket
4 fresh figs
4 slices Parma ham
4 tbsp olive oil
1 tbsp fresh orange juice
1 tbsp clear honey
1 small fresh red chilli

1 Tear the rocket into bite-sized pieces, if large, and arrange on 4 large serving plates.

2 Using a sharp knife, cut each of the figs into quarters and place them on top of the rocket.

3 Using a sharp knife, cut the Parma ham into strips and scatter over the rocket and figs.

4 Place the oil, orange juice and honey in a screw-top jar and shake until the mixture emulsifies and forms a thick dressing. Pour into a small bowl.

5 Using a sharp knife, dice the chilli, remembering not to touch your face before you have washed your hands (see cook's tip). Add the chopped chilli to the dressing and mix well.

6 Drizzle the dressing over the Parma ham, rocket and figs, tossing to mix well. Serve immediately.

NUTRITION

Calories *121*; Sugars *6 g*; Protein *1 g*; Carbohydrate *6 g*; Fat *11 g*; Saturates *2 g*

very easy

15 mins

5 mins

🍲 COOK'S TIP

Chillies can burn the skin for several hours after chopping, so it is advisable to wear gloves when you are handling the very hot varieties.

Deep-fried seafood is popular all around the Mediterranean, where fish of all kinds is fresh and abundant. Serve with Garlic Mayonnaise and lemon wedges, if you wish.

Crispy Golden Seafood

1 Carefully rinse the squid, prawns and whitebait under cold running water, completely removing any accumulated dirt or grit.

2 Using a sharp knife, slice the squid into thick rings, but leave all the tentacles whole.

3 Heat the oil in a large saucepan to 180°–190°C/350°–375°F, or until a cube of bread browns in 30 seconds.

4 Place the flour in a large bowl and season to taste with salt, pepper and the dried basil.

5 Toss the squid, prawns and whitebait in the seasoned flour until coated thoroughly all over. Carefully shake off any excess flour.

6 Cook the seafood, in batches, in the hot oil for 2–3 minutes, or until crispy and golden all over. Remove each batch of seafood with a slotted spoon and leave to drain thoroughly on kitchen paper.

7 Transfer the deep-fried seafood to 4 large serving plates and serve with the Garlic Mayonnaise (see Cook's Tip).

SERVES 4

200 g/7 oz prepared squid
200 g/7 oz raw blue tiger prawns, peeled
150 g/5½ oz whitebait
300 ml/10 fl oz oil for deep-frying
50 g/1¾ oz plain flour
1 tsp dried basil
salt and pepper
Garlic Mayonnaise, to serve (see Cook's Tip)

NUTRITION
Calories *393*; Sugars *0.2 g*; Protein *27 g*; Carbohydrate *12 g*; Fat *26 g*; Saturates *3 g*

 easy

 5 mins

15 mins

🍳 COOK'S TIP

To make the Garlic Mayonnaise, crush 2 garlic cloves, stir into 8 tablespoons of mayonnaise and season to taste with salt and pepper and 1 tablespoon of chopped fresh parsley. Cover and chill in the refrigerator until ready to serve.

This soup of mussels, cooked in white wine with onions and cream, can be served as an appetiser or a main dish with plenty of crusty bread.

Mussels *in* White Wine

SERVES 4

about 3 litres/5¼ pints fresh mussels
55 g/2 oz butter
1 large onion, chopped very finely
2–3 garlic cloves, crushed
350 ml/12 fl oz dry white wine
150 ml/5 fl oz water
2 tbsp lemon juice
good pinch of finely grated lemon rind
1 bouquet garni
1 tbsp plain flour
4 tbsp single or double cream
2–3 tbsp chopped fresh parsley
salt and pepper
crusty bread, to serve

1 Pull off all the 'beards' from the mussels and scrub them thoroughly under cold running water for about 5 minutes to remove all mud, sand and barnacles etc. Discard any mussels that refuse to close when sharply tapped with a knife.

2 Melt half the butter in a large saucepan over a low heat. Add the onion and garlic and fry gently until softened, but not coloured.

3 Add the wine, water, lemon juice and rind and bouquet garni. Season to taste with salt and pepper. Bring to the boil over a low heat, then cover and simmer for 4–5 minutes.

4 Add the mussels to the saucepan, cover tightly and simmer for 5 minutes, shaking the pan frequently, until all the mussels have opened. Discard any mussels that have not opened. Remove the bouquet garni and discard.

5 Remove the empty half shell from each mussel. Blend the remaining butter with the flour and whisk into the liquid, a little at a time. Simmer gently for 2–3 minutes, or until slightly thickened.

6 Add the cream and half the parsley to the soup and reheat gently. Adjust the seasoning, if necessary. Ladle the mussels and liquid into 4 large, warmed soup bowls, sprinkle with the remaining parsley and serve with crusty bread.

NUTRITION

Calories *396*; Sugars *2 g*; Protein *23 g*;
Carbohydrate *8 g*; Fat *24 g*; Saturates *15 g*

moderate

5–10 mins

25 mins

Sandwiches are always a welcome snack, but can be mundane. These crisp rolls filled with roasted peppers and cheese are irresistible.

Ciabatta Rolls

1 Slice the ciabatta rolls in half. Heat the olive oil and garlic in a saucepan over a low heat, then pour the garlic and oil mixture over the cut surfaces of the rolls. Reserve.

2 To make the filling, halve and deseed all the peppers, then place, skin-side up, on a grill rack. Cook under a preheated hot grill for 8–10 minutes, or until just starting to char. Remove the peppers and place in a polythene bag, then leave to cool. When cool enough to handle, peel and slice thinly.

3 Arrange the radish slices on 1 half of each roll with a few watercress leaves. Spoon the cream cheese on top. Pile the roasted peppers on top of the cream cheese and top with the other half of the roll. Serve immediately.

SERVES 4

4 ciabatta rolls
2 tbsp olive oil
1 garlic clove, crushed

filling
1 red pepper
1 green pepper
1 yellow pepper
4 radishes, sliced
1 bunch watercress
115 g/4 oz cream cheese

NUTRITION
Calories *328*; Sugars *6 g*; Protein *8 g*;
Carbohydrate *34 g*; Fat *19 g*; Saturates *9 g*

 easy
 15 mins
🕐 10 mins

🍳 **COOK'S TIP**

If you do not like the taste of green pepper, use an orange one instead.

This tasty Chinese starter is not all that it seems – the 'seaweed' is in fact pak choi, which is deep-fried, salted and tossed with toasted pine kernels.

Crispy Seaweed

SERVES 4

1 kg/2 lb 4 oz pak choi leaves
850 ml/1½ pints groundnut oil for deep-frying
1 tsp salt
1 tbsp caster sugar
2½ tbsp toasted pine kernels

1 Place the pak choi leaves in a colander and rinse under cold running water, then pat dry thoroughly with kitchen paper.

2 Discard any tough outer leaves and roll each pak choi leaf up, then, using a sharp knife, slice through thinly so the leaves are finely shredded. Alternatively, use a food processor to shred the pak choi.

3 Heat the oil in a preheated wok or large saucepan over a medium heat.

4 Carefully add the shredded pak choi leaves to the wok or saucepan and fry for about 30 seconds, or until they shrivel up and become crispy, resembling seaweed (you will probably need to do this in several batches, depending on the size of your wok or frying pan).

5 Remove the crispy seaweed from the wok or saucepan with a slotted spoon and drain on kitchen paper.

6 Transfer the crispy seaweed to a large bowl and toss with the salt, sugar and pine kernels. Transfer to 4 warmed serving plates and serve immediately.

NUTRITION
Calories 214; Sugars 14 g; Protein 6 g; Carbohydrate 15 g; Fat 15 g; Saturates 2 g

⭐ very easy
🕐 10 mins
🕐 5 mins

👨‍🍳 **COOK'S TIP**

The tough outer leaves of pak choi are discarded as these will spoil the overall taste and texture of the dish. Use Savoy cabbage instead of the pak choi if it is unavailable, drying the leaves thoroughly before frying.

Polenta can be found in most supermarkets or health food shops. Yellow in colour, it acts as a binding agent in this recipe.

Spicy Sweetcorn Fritters

1 Place the sweetcorn, chillies, garlic, lime leaves, coriander, egg and polenta in a large mixing bowl, and stir thoroughly.

2 Add the French beans to the bowl and, using a wooden spoon, mix well.

3 Divide the mixture into small, evenly sized balls, then flatten the balls of mixture gently between the palms of your hands to form rounds.

4 Heat the groundnut oil in a preheated wok or large frying pan until really hot. Cook the fritters in batches, turning occasionally, until brown and crispy on the outside.

5 Remove the cooked fritters from the wok or frying pan with a slotted spoon and leave to drain on kitchen paper while frying the remaining fritters.

6 Transfer the fritters to 4 warmed serving plates and serve immediately.

SERVES 4

225 g/8 oz canned or frozen sweetcorn kernels

2 fresh red chillies, deseeded and finely chopped

2 garlic cloves, crushed

10 kaffir lime leaves, chopped finely

2 tbsp chopped fresh coriander

1 large egg

75 g/2¾ oz polenta

100 g/3½ oz French beans, sliced finely

150 ml/5 fl oz groundnut oil for deep-frying

NUTRITION
Calories *213*; Sugars *6 g*; Protein *5 g*;
Carbohydrate *30 g*; Fat *8 g*; Saturates *1 g*

⭐⭐   easy

🕐   5 mins

🕐   15 mins

This classic Chinese appetizer is also a great nibble for serving at parties – but be sure to make plenty!

Pork Sesame Toasts

SERVES 4

250 g/9 oz lean pork
250 g/9 oz raw prawns, peeled and deveined
4 spring onions, trimmed
1 garlic clove, crushed
1 tbsp chopped fresh coriander leaves and stems
1 tbsp Thai fish sauce
1 egg, beaten
8–10 slices of thick-cut white bread
3 tbsp sesame seeds
150 ml/5 fl oz vegetable oil
salt and pepper

to garnish
fresh coriander sprigs
½ red pepper, sliced finely

NUTRITION

Calories *674*; Sugars *2 g*; Protein *33 g*;
Carbohydrate *33 g*; Fat *46 g*; Saturates *7 g*

easy

5 mins

35 mins

1 Place the pork, prawns, spring onions, garlic, coriander, Thai fish sauce and egg in a food processor or blender. Season to taste with salt and pepper and process for a few seconds until the ingredients are finely chopped. Transfer the mixture to a bowl. Alternatively, chop the pork, prawns and spring onions very finely, then add the garlic, chopped coriander, Thai fish sauce and egg. Season to taste with salt and pepper and mix until blended.

2 Spread the pork and prawn mixture thickly over the slices of bread so it reaches up to the edges. Cut off the crusts and slice each piece of bread into 4 squares or triangles.

3 Sprinkle the topping liberally with sesame seeds.

4 Heat the vegetable oil in a preheated wok or frying pan over a medium heat. Add a few pieces of the bread and fry, topping side down first, so the egg sets, for about 2 minutes, or until golden brown. Turn the pieces over to cook on the other side, about 1 minute.

5 Remove the toasts from the wok or frying pan and drain on kitchen paper. Fry the remaining pieces. Arrange the toasts on a serving plate, garnish with fresh coriander sprigs and strips of red pepper and serve.

Chunks of chicken breast are marinated in a mixture of lime juice, garlic, sesame oil and fresh ginger to give them a great flavour.

Sesame Ginger Chicken

1 To make the marinade, place the garlic, shallot, sesame oil, Thai fish sauce or soy sauce, lime or lemon rind and juice, sesame seeds, grated ginger and mint in a large non-metallic bowl. Season with a little salt and pepper and stir well until all the ingredients are mixed thoroughly.

2 Remove the skin from the chicken breasts and discard. Using a sharp knife, cut the flesh into chunks.

3 Add the chicken to the marinade, stirring to coat the chicken completely in the mixture. Cover with clingfilm and chill in the refrigerator for at least 2 hours, so all the flavours are absorbed.

4 Thread the chicken on to 4 presoaked wooden satay sticks. Place them on the rack of a grill pan and baste with the marinade.

5 Place the kebabs under a preheated hot grill for about 8–10 minutes. Turn them frequently, basting them with the remaining marinade.

6 Put the chicken kebabs on to a large serving plate, garnish with a mint sprig and serve immediately with a dipping sauce.

SERVES 4

500 g/1 lb 2 oz boneless chicken breasts
1 fresh mint sprig, to garnish
dipping sauce, to serve

marinade
1 garlic clove, crushed
1 shallot, chopped very finely
2 tbsp sesame oil
1 tbsp Thai fish sauce or light soy sauce
finely grated rind of 1 lime or ½ lemon
2 tbsp lime juice or lemon juice
1 tsp sesame seeds
2 tsp finely grated fresh root ginger
2 tsp chopped fresh mint
salt and pepper

NUTRITION
Calories *204*; Sugars *0 g*; Protein *28 g*; Carbohydrate *1 g*; Fat *10 g*; Saturates *2 g*

 easy

 2 hrs 15 mins

10 mins

🍲 **COOK'S TIP**

These chicken kebabs taste delicious if they are dipped into an accompanying bowl of hot chilli sauce.

For the best results, use raw tiger prawns in their shells. They are about 7–10 cm/2¾–4 inches long, and you should get 18–20 per 500 g/1 lb 2 oz.

Spicy Salt *and* Pepper Prawns

SERVES 4

250–300 g/9–10½ oz raw prawns in their shells, thawed if frozen
1 tbsp light soy sauce
1 tsp Chinese rice wine or dry sherry
2 tsp cornflour
300 ml/10 fl oz vegetable oil for deep-frying
2–3 spring onions, to garnish

spicy salt and pepper
1 tbsp salt
1 tsp ground Szechuan peppercorns
1 tsp Chinese five-spice powder

1 Pull the soft legs off the prawns, but keep the body shell on. Dry thoroughly on kitchen paper.

2 Place the prawns in a bowl with the soy sauce, Chinese rice wine or sherry and cornflour. Coat the prawns in the mixture, cover and leave to marinate in the refrigerator for about 25–30 minutes.

3 To make the spicy salt and pepper, mix the salt, Szechuan peppercorns and Chinese five-spice powder together in a small bowl. Place in a dry frying pan and stir-fry for 3–4 minutes over a low heat, stirring constantly, to prevent the spices burning on the base of the pan. Remove from the heat and leave to cool.

4 Heat the vegetable oil in a preheated wok or large frying pan until smoking. Add the prawns, in batches, and deep-fry until golden brown. Remove the prawns from the wok with a slotted spoon and drain on kitchen paper.

5 Place the spring onions in a bowl, pour on 1 tablespoon of the hot oil and leave for 30 seconds. Transfer the prawns to a large serving plate and garnish with the spring onions. Serve with the spicy salt and pepper as a dip.

NUTRITION
Calories *160*; Sugars *0.2 g*; Protein *17 g*;
Carbohydrate *0.5 g*; Fat *10 g*; Saturates *1 g*

 moderate
 35 mins
35 mins
20 mins

(☺) **COOK'S TIP**

The roasted spice mixture made with Szechuan peppercorns is used throughout China as a dip for deep-fried food. The peppercorns are sometimes roasted first, then ground. Dry-frying releases the flavours of the spices.

Serve as a starter, or simply spread on small pieces of toasted crusty bread (crostini) as an appetizer with drinks.

Crostini *alla* Fiorentina

1 Heat the olive oil in a frying pan over a low heat. Add the onion, celery, carrot and garlic and cook gently for 4–5 minutes.

2 Meanwhile, rinse the chicken livers and pat dry on kitchen paper. Rinse the calf's or other liver and pat dry. Slice into strips. Add the liver to the pan and fry gently for a few minutes until the strips are well sealed on all sides.

3 Add half the wine and cook until it has mostly evaporated. Add the rest of the wine, tomato purée, half the parsley, anchovies, stock or water, a little salt and plenty of pepper.

4 Cover the pan and simmer, stirring occasionally, for 15–20 minutes, or until tender and most of the liquid has been absorbed.

5 Leave the mixture to cool slightly, then either coarsely mince or put into a food processor and process to a chunky purée.

6 Return to the pan and add the butter, capers and remaining parsley. Heat through gently until the butter melts. Adjust the seasoning, if necessary and spoon into a bowl. Garnish with chopped parsley and serve warm or cold spread on slices of toasted crusty bread.

SERVES 4

3 tbsp olive oil
1 onion, chopped
1 celery stick, chopped
1 carrot, chopped
1–2 garlic cloves, crushed
125 g/4½ oz chicken livers
125 g/4½ oz calf's, lamb's or pig's liver
150 ml/5 fl oz red wine
1 tbsp tomato purée
2 tbsp chopped fresh parsley
3–4 canned anchovy fillets, chopped finely
2 tbsp stock or water
25–40 g/1–1½ oz butter
1 tbsp capers, drained
salt and pepper
chopped fresh parsley, to garnish
small pieces of toasted crusty bread, to serve

NUTRITION

Calories *393*; Sugars *2 g*; Protein *17 g*; Carbohydrate *19 g*; Fat *25 g*; Saturates *9 g*

⭐⭐⭐ moderate
        10 mins
  40–45 mins

In this dish, strips of chicken or beef are threaded on to skewers, grilled and served with a spicy peanut sauce.

Chicken *or* Beef Satay

SERVES 6

4 boneless, skinless chicken breasts or
750 g/1 lb 10 oz rump steak, trimmed
lime wedges, to serve

marinade

1 small onion, chopped finely
1 garlic clove, crushed
2.5-cm/1-inch piece root ginger, grated
2 tbsp dark soy sauce
2 tsp chilli powder
1 tsp ground coriander
2 tsp dark brown sugar
1 tbsp lemon or lime juice
1 tbsp vegetable oil

peanut sauce

300 ml/10 fl oz coconut milk
4 tbsp crunchy peanut butter
1 tbsp Thai fish sauce
1 tsp lemon or lime juice
salt and pepper

NUTRITION

Calories *314*; Sugars *8 g*; Protein *32 g*;
Carbohydrate *10 g*; Fat *16 g*; Saturates *4 g*

 moderate

 2 hrs 15 mins

15 mins

1 Using a sharp knife, trim any fat from the chicken or beef and discard. Cut the meat into thin strips, about 7.5-cm/3-inches long.

2 To make the marinade, place all the ingredients in a large, shallow dish and mix well. Add the meat strips and coat well in the marinade. Cover with clingfilm and leave to marinate in the refrigerator for at least 2 hours, or preferably overnight.

3 Remove the meat from the marinade and thread the pieces, concertina style, on to presoaked bamboo or thin wooden skewers.

4 Place the satays under a preheated medium-hot grill and cook for about 8–10 minutes, turning and brushing occasionally with the marinade, until cooked through.

5 Meanwhile, to make the sauce, mix the coconut milk with the peanut butter, Thai fish sauce and lemon or lime juice in a saucepan. Bring to the boil and cook for 3 minutes. Season to taste with salt and pepper.

6 Pour the sauce into a serving bowl and serve with the cooked satays and lime wedges.

This is an ideal dish for cooks in a hurry, as it is prepared in minutes from store cupboard ingredients.

Pasta *and* Anchovy Sauce

1 Reserve 1 teaspoon of the olive oil and heat the remainder in a small saucepan over a medium heat. Add the garlic and fry for 3 minutes.

2 Reduce the heat, stir in the anchovies and cook, stirring occasionally, until the anchovies have disintegrated.

3 Bring a large saucepan of lightly salted water to the boil over a medium heat. Add the pasta and the remaining olive oil and cook for 8–10 minutes, or until just tender, but still firm to the bite.

4 Add the pesto and chopped oregano to the anchovy mixture, then season with pepper to taste.

5 Drain the pasta with a slotted spoon and transfer to a warmed serving dish. Pour the pesto mixture over the pasta, then sprinkle over the grated Parmesan cheese.

6 Garnish with fresh oregano sprigs and serve immediately with extra cheese, if you wish.

SERVES 4

6 tbsp olive oil
2 garlic cloves, crushed
55 g/2 oz canned anchovy fillets, drained
450 g/1 lb dried spaghetti
55 g/2 oz pesto
2 tbsp finely chopped fresh oregano
85 g/3 oz freshly grated Parmesan cheese, plus extra for serving (optional)
salt and pepper
2 fresh oregano sprigs, to garnish

NUTRITION
Calories 712; Sugars 4 g; Protein 25 g; Carbohydrate 81 g; Fat 34 g; Saturates 8 g

 moderate

 10 mins

25 mins

👨‍🍳 **COOK'S TIP**

If you find canned anchovy fillets rather too salty, soak them in a saucer of cold milk for 5 minutes, drain and pat dry with kitchen paper before using. The milk absorbs the salt.

Fish *and* Seafood

The wealth of species and flavours of fish that the world's oceans and rivers provide is immense. Each country combines its local catch with the region's favourite herbs and spices to create a variety of dishes. All of the recipes featured here are easy to prepare and delicious to eat. Moreover, not only are fish and seafood quick to cook, but they are also packed full with nutritional goodness. Naturally low in fat, yet rich in minerals and proteins, fish and seafood are important to help balance any diet.

The superb recipes in this chapter demonstrate the richness of cooking with fish and seafood. Dishes include modern variations of traditional recipes, such as Prawn Pasta Bake and Trout with Smoked Bacon, and exotic flavours, such as Seafood Chow Mein and Indian Cod with Tomatoes.

Seafood is plentiful in Italy and each region has its own seafood salad. The dressing needs to be chilled for several hours, so prepare well in advance.

Seafood Salad

SERVES 4

600 ml/1 pint water
150 ml/5 fl oz dry white wine
175 g/6 oz squid rings, thawed if frozen
225 g/8 oz hake or monkfish, cut into cubes
16–20 mussels, scrubbed and debearded
20 clams in shells, scrubbed
125–175 g/4½–6 oz raw prawns, peeled
3–4 spring onions, sliced (optional)
lemon wedges, to garnish
radicchio and curly endive leaves, to serve

dressing
6 tbsp olive oil
1 tbsp wine vinegar
2 tbsp chopped fresh parsley
1–2 garlic cloves, crushed
salt and pepper

garlic mayonnaise
5 tbsp thick mayonnaise
2–3 tbsp fromage frais or natural yogurt
2 garlic cloves, crushed
1 tbsp capers, drained
2 tbsp chopped fresh parsley or mixed herbs

NUTRITION
Calories *471*; Sugars *2 g*; Protein *34 g*;
Carbohydrate *4 g*; Fat *33 g*; Saturates *5 g*

moderate

45–55 mins

20–22 mins

1 Place the water and wine in a large saucepan and bring to the boil over a low heat. Add the squid and poach for 5 minutes, or until nearly tender. Add the fish and cook gently for 7–8 minutes, or until tender. Strain, reserving the fish. Pour the stock into a clean saucepan.

2 Bring the fish stock to the boil over a medium heat. Add the mussels and clams, cover and simmer gently for about 5 minutes, or until the shells open. Discard any mussels that remain closed. Drain the shellfish and remove from their shells, then put into a bowl with the cooked fish. Add the prawns and spring onions (if using).

3 To make the dressing, whisk the olive oil, vinegar, parsley and garlic together. season to taste with salt and pepper and pour over the fish, mixing well. Cover and chill in the refrigerator for several hours.

4 To make the mayonnaise, put all the ingredients into a bowl and mix until blended. Cover and chill in the refrigerator until ready to serve.

5 Arrange the radicchio and curly endive on 4 serving plates and spoon the fish salad into the centre. Garnish with lemon wedges and serve with the garlic mayonnaise.

🍳 COOK'S TIP

You could substitute cooked scallops for the mussels and cockles for the clams, if you prefer.

The combination of chargrilled peppers and mussels makes this an ideal starter or a light lunch on a hot summer's day. Serve with plenty of crusty bread.

Mussel Salad

1 Place the peppers, skin-side up, on a grill rack and cook under a preheated hot grill for 8–10 minutes, or until the skin is charred and blistered and the flesh is soft. Remove from the grill with tongs, place in a bowl and cover with clingfilm. Leave to cool for about 10 minutes, then peel off the skins.

2 Slice the pepper flesh into thin strips and place in a bowl. Gently stir in the shelled mussels.

3 To make the dressing, whisk the olive oil, lemon juice and rind, honey, mustard and chives together in a bowl until well blended. Season to taste with salt and pepper, then add the pepper and mussel mixture and toss gently until coated.

4 Remove the central core of the radicchio and shred the leaves. Place in a serving bowl with the rocket and toss together.

5 Pile the mussel mixture into the centre of the leaves and arrange the green-lipped mussels in their shells around the edge of the bowl. Garnish with lemon rind and serve with crusty bread.

SERVES 4

2 large red peppers, halved and deseeded
350 g/12 oz cooked shelled mussels, thawed if frozen
1 head of radicchio
25 g/1 oz rocket
8 cooked green-lipped mussels in their shells
strips of lemon rind, to garnish
crusty bread, to serve

dressing
1 tbsp olive oil
1 tbsp lemon juice
1 tsp finely grated lemon rind
2 tsp clear honey
1 tsp French mustard
1 tbsp snipped fresh chives
salt and pepper

NUTRITION
Calories *181*; Sugars *3.5 g*; Protein *18 g*;
Carbohydrate *11.3 g*; Fat *10.4 g*; Saturates *3 g*

 easy

 15 mins

10 mins

Flageolet beans, courgettes and tomatoes are briefly cooked in a sweet and sour sauce, before being mixed with the tuna.

Sweet *and* Sour Tuna Salad

SERVES 4

2 tbsp olive oil
1 onion, chopped
2 garlic cloves, chopped
2 courgettes, sliced
4 tomatoes, peeled
400 g/14 oz canned flageolet beans, drained and rinsed
10 stoned black olives, halved
1 tbsp capers, drained
1 tsp caster sugar
1 tbsp wholegrain mustard
1 tbsp white wine vinegar
200 g/7 oz canned tuna, drained
2 tbsp chopped fresh parsley, plus extra to garnish
crusty bread, to serve

1 Heat the olive oil in a large, heavy-based frying pan over a low heat. Add the onion and garlic and fry, stirring occasionally, for 5 minutes, or until softened, but not browned.

2 Add the courgette and cook, stirring occasionally, for a further 3 minutes.

3 Cut the tomatoes in half, then into thin wedges.

4 Add the tomatoes to the pan with the flageolet beans, olives, capers, sugar, mustard and vinegar.

5 Simmer for 2 minutes, stirring gently, then leave to cool slightly.

6 Flake the tuna and stir it into the bean mixture with the chopped parsley. Transfer to 4 serving plates, garnish with the extra chopped parsley and serve warm with crusty bread.

NUTRITION
Calories *245*; Sugars *5 g*; Protein *22 g*;
Carbohydrate *24 g*; Fat *8 g*; Saturates *1 g*

★★   easy
    15 mins
🕐   10 mins

🍴 **COOK'S TIP**

Capers are the flower buds of the caper bush, which is native to the Mediterranean region. Capers are preserved in vinegar and salt and give a distinctive flavour to this salad. They are used in Italian and Provençal cooking.

Smoked trout and horseradish are natural partners, but with apple and watercress this makes a wonderful first course.

Smoked Trout *and* Apple Salad

1 Leaving the skin on, cut the apples into quarters and remove the cores. Slice the apples into a bowl and toss in the French dressing to prevent them turning brown.

2 Break the watercress into sprigs and arrange on 4 serving plates.

3 Skin the trout and take out the bone. Carefully remove any fine bones that remain, using your fingers or tweezers. Flake the trout into fairly large pieces and arrange with the apple between the watercress.

4 To make the horseradish dressing, whisk all the ingredients together, adding a little milk if too thick, then drizzle over the trout. Sprinkle the snipped chives and flowers (if using) over the trout and serve with the Melba Toast (see Cook's Tip).

SERVES 4

2 orange-red eating apples
2 tbsp French dressing
½ bunch watercress
1 smoked trout, about 175 g/6 oz
Melba Toast, to serve (see Cook's Tip)

horseradish dressing
125 ml/4 fl oz low-fat natural yogurt
½–1 tsp lemon juice
1 tbsp horseradish sauce
milk, optional
salt and pepper

to garnish
1 tbsp snipped fresh chives
fresh chive flowers, optional

NUTRITION

Calories *133*; Sugars *11 g*; Protein *12 g*; Carbohydrate *11 g*; Fat *5 g*; Saturates *1 g*

 very easy

 10 mins

◷ 20 mins

☻ COOK'S TIP

To make the Melba Toast, toast medium sliced bread, then cut off the crusts and slice in half horizontally. Cut in half diagonally and place toasted side down in a warmed oven for 15–20 minutes until the edges start to curl.

Serve as part of a selection of antipasti, or for a summer lunch with hot garlic bread. Tuna and beans make a classic combination.

Tuna, Bean *and* Anchovy Salad

SERVES 4

500 g/1 lb 2 oz tomatoes
200 g/7 oz canned tuna, drained
2 tbsp chopped fresh parsley
½ cucumber
1 small red onion
225 g/8 oz cooked green beans
1 small red pepper, deseeded
1 small crisp lettuce
6 tbsp Italian-style dressing
3 hard-boiled eggs
55 g/2 oz canned anchovy fillets drained
12 stoned black olives

1 Cut the tomatoes into wedges, flake the tuna and put both into a small bowl with the chopped parsley.

2 Cut the cucumber into slices. Thinly slice the onion, then add the cucumber and onion to the bowl.

3 Cut the green beans in half, chop the pepper and add both to the bowl with the lettuce. Pour over the dressing and toss to mix well, then spoon into a salad bowl. Shell the eggs and cut into quarters. Add to the salad with the anchovies, then scatter over the olives and serve.

NUTRITION

Calories *397*; Sugars *8 g*; Protein *23 g*;
Carbohydrate *10 g*; Fat *30 g*; Saturates *4 g*

⭐   very easy

      20 mins

      0 mins

A lemon and herb sauce perfectly complements the sweet flavour and delicate texture of the fish.

Fillets *of* Red Mullet *and* Pasta

1 Place the red mullet fillets in a large casserole dish. Pour over the wine and add the shallots, garlic, herbs, lemon rind and juice, nutmeg and anchovies. Season to taste with salt and pepper. Cover the casserole and bake in a preheated oven at 180°C/350°F/Gas Mark 4, for 35 minutes.

2 Transfer the baked mullet fillets carefully to a warmed dish and reserve. Keep warm.

3 Pour the cooking liquid into a saucepan and bring to the boil over a low heat. Mix the cream and cornflour together in a small bowl and stir into the sauce to thicken.

4 Meanwhile, bring a saucepan of lightly salted water to the boil over a medium heat. Add the pasta and olive oil and cook for 8–10 minutes, or until tender, but still firm to the bite. Drain the pasta and transfer to a warmed serving dish.

5 Arrange the red mullet fillets on top of the pasta and pour over the sauce. Garnish with a mint sprig, a few slices of lemon and strips of lemon rind. Serve immediately.

 COOK'S TIP

If you cannot find red mullet fillets, use whatever fish is available, such as trout or red snapper.

SERVES 4

1 kg/2 lb 4 oz red mullet fillets
300 ml/10 fl oz dry white wine
4 shallots, chopped finely
1 garlic clove, crushed
3 tbsp finely chopped mixed fresh herbs
finely grated rind and juice of 1 lemon
pinch of freshly grated nutmeg
3 canned anchovy fillets, chopped roughly
2 tbsp double cream
1 tsp cornflour
450 g/1 lb dried vermicelli
1 tsp olive oil
salt and pepper

to garnish
1 fresh mint sprig
lemon slices
lemon rind strips

NUTRITION
Calories *457*; Sugars *3 g*; Protein *39 g*;
Carbohydrate *44 g*; Fat *12 g*; Saturates *5 g*

⭐⭐⭐   moderate

🕐   15 mins

🕐   1 hr

Most trout available nowadays is farmed rainbow trout. However, if you can, buy wild brown trout for this recipe.

Trout *with* Smoked Bacon

SERVES 4

1 tbsp butter for greasing
4 trout, about 275 g/9½ oz each, gutted and cleaned
12 canned anchovy fillets in oil, drained and chopped
2 apples, peeled, cored and sliced
4 fresh mint sprigs
juice of 1 lemon
12 slices rindless smoked streaky bacon
450 g/1 lb dried tagliatelle
1 tsp olive oil
salt and pepper

to garnish

2 apples, cored and sliced
4 fresh mint sprigs

NUTRITION

Calories *802*; Sugars *8 g*; Protein *68 g*;
Carbohydrate *54 g*; Fat *36 g*; Saturates *10 g*

 challenging

35 mins

25 mins

1 Grease a deep baking tray with the butter.

2 Open up the cavities of each trout and rinse with warm salt water. Season each cavity with salt and pepper. Divide the anchovies, apples and mint between each of the cavities, then sprinkle the lemon juice into each cavity.

3 Carefully cover the whole of each trout, except the head and tail, with 3 slices of smoked bacon in a spiral shape.

4 Arrange the trout on the prepared baking tray with the loose ends of bacon tucked underneath. Season with pepper to taste and bake in a preheated oven at 200°C/400°F/Gas Mark 6, for 20 minutes, turning the trout over after 10 minutes.

5 Meanwhile, bring a large saucepan of lightly salted water to the boil over a medium heat. Add the pasta and olive oil and cook for about 10–12 minutes, or until tender, but still firm to the bite. Drain the pasta and transfer to a large, warmed serving dish.

6 Remove the trout from the oven and arrange on top of the pasta. Garnish with sliced apples and mint sprigs and serve immediately.

Fresh salmon and pasta
in a mouthwatering lemon
and watercress sauce –
a wonderful summer
evening treat.

Salmon Steaks *with* Penne

1 Place the salmon in a large frying pan. Add the butter, wine, sea salt, the peppercorns, dill, tarragon and lemon. Cover, bring to the boil over a low heat and simmer for 10 minutes.

2 Using a fish slice, carefully remove the salmon. Strain and reserve the cooking liquid. Remove the salmon skin and centre bones and discard. Place in a warmed dish, cover and keep warm.

3 Meanwhile, bring a large saucepan of lightly salted water to the boil over a medium heat. Add the pasta and 1 teaspoon of the olive oil and cook for about 12 minutes, or until tender, but still firm to the bite. Drain and sprinkle over the remaining olive oil. Place in a warmed serving dish, top with the salmon steaks and keep warm.

4 To make the sauce, melt the butter over a low heat, then stir in the flour for 2 minutes. Stir in the milk and 7 tablespoons of the reserved cooking liquid. Add the lemon juice and rind and cook, stirring, for a further 10 minutes.

5 Add the watercress to the sauce, stir gently and season to taste with salt and pepper.

6 Pour the sauce over the salmon and pasta, garnish with lemon slices and watercress and serve immediately.

SERVES 4

4 fresh salmon steaks, 280 g/10 oz each
55 g/2 oz butter
175 ml/6 fl oz dry white wine
pinch of sea salt
8 peppercorns
1 fresh dill sprig
1 fresh tarragon sprig
1 lemon, sliced
450 g/1 lb dried penne
1 tbsp olive oil

lemon & watercress sauce
25 g/1 oz butter
25 g/1 oz plain flour
150 ml/5 fl oz warm milk
juice and finely grated rind of 2 lemons
55 g/2 oz watercress, chopped
salt and pepper

to garnish
lemon slices
fresh watercress

NUTRITION
Calories *968*; Sugars *3 g*; Protein *59 g*; Carbohydrate *49 g*; Fat *58 g*; Saturates *19 g*

 easy

 10 mins

10 mins

30 mins

This dish is ideal for an easy family supper. You can use whatever pasta you like, but the tricolour varieties will give the most colourful results.

Prawn Pasta Bake

SERVES 4

225 g/8 oz dried tricolour pasta shapes
1 tbsp vegetable oil
175 g/6 oz button mushrooms, sliced
1 bunch spring onions, trimmed
 and chopped
400 g/14 oz canned tuna in brine,
 drained and flaked
175 g/6 oz peeled prawns, thawed if frozen
2 tbsp cornflour
425 ml/15 fl oz skimmed milk
4 medium tomatoes, sliced thinly
25 g/1 oz fresh breadcrumbs
25 g/1 oz freshly grated reduced-fat
 Cheddar cheese
salt and pepper

1 Bring a large saucepan of lightly salted water to the boil over a medium heat. Add the pasta and cook for 8–10 minutes, or until tender, but still firm to the bite. Drain thoroughly.

2 Meanwhile, heat the oil in a large frying pan over a low heat. Add the mushrooms and all but a handful of the spring onions and cook, stirring occasionally, for 4–5 minutes, or until softened.

3 Place the cooked pasta in a small bowl and stir in the mushroom mixture, tuna and prawns.

4 Blend the cornflour with a little milk to make a paste. Pour the remaining milk into a saucepan and stir in the paste. Heat, stirring, until the sauce starts to thicken. Season well with salt and pepper. Stir the sauce into the pasta mixture, then transfer to an ovenproof dish and place on a baking tray.

5 Arrange the tomato slices over the pasta and sprinkle with the breadcrumbs and grated cheese. Bake in a preheated oven at 190°C/375°F/Gas Mark 5, for 25–30 minutes until golden. Sprinkle with the reserved spring onions and serve immediately.

NUTRITION

Calories 723; Sugars 9 g; Protein 56 g;
Carbohydrate 114 g; Fat 8 g; Saturates 2 g

 easy

10 mins

50 mins

Use whatever seafood is available for this delicious noodle dish – mussels or crab would be suitable.

Seafood Chow Mein

1 Open up the squid and score the inside in a criss-cross pattern, then cut into pieces about the size of a postage stamp. Soak the squid in a bowl of boiling water until all the pieces curl up. Rinse in cold water and drain.

2 Cut each scallop into 3–4 slices. Cut the prawns in half lengthways, if large. Blend the cornflour with a little water to make a paste. Mix the scallops and prawns together with the egg white and cornflour paste.

3 Bring a large saucepan of water to the boil over a medium heat. Add the noodles and cook for 5–6 minutes. Drain and rinse under cold running water. Drain again, then toss with about 1 tablespoon of vegetable oil.

4 Heat 3 tablespoons of vegetable oil in a preheated wok over a medium heat. Add the noodles and 1 tablespoon of the soy sauce and stir-fry for about 2–3 minutes. Transfer to a large serving dish.

5 Heat the remaining oil in the wok and add the mangetout and seafood. Stir-fry for 2 minutes, then add the salt, sugar, wine, remaining soy sauce and about half the spring onions. Blend well and add a little water, if necessary. Pour the mixture on top of the noodles and sprinkle with sesame oil. Garnish with the remaining spring onions and serve.

 COOK'S TIP

Chinese rice wine, made from glutinous rice, is also known as 'Yellow wine' because of its golden amber colour. If it is unavailable, a good dry or medium sherry is an acceptable substitute.

SERVES 4

90 g/3¼ oz squid, cleaned
3–4 fresh scallops
90 g/3¼ oz raw prawns, peeled
1 tbsp cornflour
½ egg white, beaten lightly
275 g/9½ oz egg noodles
5–6 tbsp vegetable oil
2 tbsp light soy sauce
55 g/2 oz mangetout
½ tsp salt
½ tsp sugar
1 tsp Chinese rice wine
2 spring onions, shredded finely
few drops of sesame oil

NUTRITION

Calories 281; Sugars 1 g; Protein 15 g; Carbohydrate 16 g; Fat 18 g; Saturates 2 g

⭐⭐⭐ moderate
🕐 15 mins
🕐 15 mins

This delicious dish combines sweet and sour flavours with the addition of egg, rice noodles, king prawns and vegetables for a real treat.

Sweet *and* Sour Noodles

SERVES 4

3 tbsp Thai fish sauce
2 tbsp distilled white vinegar
2 tbsp caster or palm sugar
2 tbsp tomato purée
2 tbsp sunflower oil
3 garlic cloves, crushed
350 g/12 oz rice noodles, soaked in boiling
    water for 5 minutes
8 spring onions, sliced
175 g/6 oz carrot, grated
150 g/5½ oz bean sprouts
2 eggs, beaten
225 g/8 oz peeled king prawns
50 g/1¾ oz chopped peanuts
1 tsp chilli flakes, to garnish

1 Mix the Thai fish sauce, vinegar, sugar and tomato purée together in a bowl.

2 Heat the sunflower oil in a large preheated wok over a low heat, then add the garlic and stir-fry for 30 seconds.

3 Drain the noodles thoroughly and add them to the wok together with the fish sauce and tomato purée mixture. Mix well.

4 Add the spring onions, carrot and bean sprouts to the wok and stir-fry for 2–3 minutes.

5 Move the stir-fry mixture to one side of the wok, add the beaten eggs to the empty part of the wok and cook until the egg sets. Add the prawns and peanuts to the wok and mix well. Transfer to 4 warmed serving dishes and garnish with chilli flakes. Serve immediately.

NUTRITION
Calories *352*; Sugars *14 g*; Protein *23 g*;
Carbohydrate *29 g*; Fat *17 g*; Saturates *3 g*

  moderate

  10 mins

10 mins

🍳 **COOK'S TIP**

Chilli flakes may be found in the spice section of large supermarkets. If they are unavailable, use crushed chillies instead.

Cellophane or 'glass' noodles are made from mung beans. They are sold dried, so they need soaking before use.

Chilli Prawn Noodles

1 Mix the light soy sauce, lime or lemon juice and fish sauce together in a small bowl. Add the tofu chunks and toss them until well coated in the mixture. Cover with clingfilm and leave for 15 minutes.

2 Place the noodles in a large bowl and pour over enough warm water to cover. Leave to soak for about 5 minutes, then drain well.

3 Heat the sesame oil in a wok or large frying pan over a low heat. Add the shallots, garlic and chilli and stir-fry for 1 minute.

4 Add the sliced celery and carrots and stir-fry for a further 2–3 minutes.

5 Tip the drained noodles into the wok or frying pan and cook, stirring constantly, for 2 minutes, then add the prawns, bean sprouts and tofu with the soy sauce mixture. Cook over a medium-high heat for 2–3 minutes, or until heated through.

6 Transfer the mixture to 4 warmed serving dishes, garnish with celery leaves and chillies and serve.

SERVES 4

2 tbsp light soy sauce
1 tbsp lime or lemon juice
1 tbsp Thai fish sauce
125 g/4½ oz firm tofu, cut into chunks (drained weight)
125 g/4½ oz cellophane noodles
2 tbsp sesame oil
4 shallots, sliced finely
2 garlic cloves, crushed
1 small fresh red chilli, deseeded and finely chopped
2 celery sticks, sliced finely
2 carrots, sliced finely
125 g/4½ oz cooked, peeled prawns
55 g/2 oz bean sprouts

to garnish
celery leaves
fresh chillies

NUTRITION
Calories *152*; Sugars *2 g*; Protein *11 g*; Carbohydrate *10 g*; Fat *8 g*; Saturates *1 g*

  moderate
25 mins
10 mins

(🍳) COOK'S TIP

Try using raw tiger prawns instead of the cooked prawns and add them to the wok with the celery in step 4.

Fish and fruit are tossed with a trio of peppers in this spicy dish served with noodles for a quick, healthy meal.

Noodles *with* Cod *and* Mango

SERVES 4

250 g/9 oz egg noodles
450 g/1 lb skinless cod fillet
1 tbsp paprika
2 tbsp sunflower oil
1 red onion, sliced
1 orange pepper, deseeded and sliced
1 green pepper, deseeded and sliced
100 g/3½ oz baby sweetcorn, halved
1 mango, peeled, stoned and sliced
100 g/3½ oz bean sprouts
2 tbsp tomato ketchup
2 tbsp soy sauce
2 tbsp medium sherry
1 tsp cornflour

1 Place the egg noodles in a large bowl and pour over enough boiling water to cover. Leave to stand for about 10 minutes.

2 Rinse the cod fillet under cold running water and pat dry with kitchen paper. Cut the cod flesh into thin strips, then place in a large bowl. Add the paprika and toss well to coat the fish.

3 Heat the sunflower oil in a large preheated wok over a medium heat. Add the onion, peppers and baby sweetcorn and stir-fry for about 5 minutes.

4 Add the cod to the wok together with the sliced mango and stir-fry for a further 2–3 minutes, or until the fish is tender. Add the bean sprouts and toss well.

5 Mix the tomato ketchup, soy sauce, sherry and cornflour together in a small bowl. Add the mixture to the wok and cook, stirring occasionally, until the juices thicken.

6 Drain the noodles thoroughly and transfer to 4 warmed serving bowls. Transfer the cod and mango stir-fry to separate warmed serving bowls and serve immediately.

NUTRITION

Calories *274*; Sugars *11 g*; Protein *25 g*; Carbohydrate *26 g*; Fat *8 g*; Saturates *1 g*

    easy

10 mins

25 mins

Chicken and noodles are cooked, then tossed in an oyster sauce and egg mixture in this delicious recipe.

Oyster Sauce Noodles

1 Place the egg noodles in a large bowl or dish and pour over enough boiling water to cover. Leave to stand for 10 minutes.

2 Meanwhile, remove the skin from the chicken thighs and discard. Cut the chicken flesh into small pieces with a sharp knife.

3 Heat the groundnut oil in a large preheated wok or frying pan, swirling the oil around the base of the wok until it is really hot.

4 Add the chicken pieces and the carrot slices to the wok or frying pan and stir-fry for about 5 minutes.

5 Drain the noodles thoroughly, then add to the wok. Stir-fry for a further 2–3 minutes, or until the noodles are heated through.

6 Beat the oyster sauce, eggs and water together. Drizzle the mixture over the noodles and stir-fry for a further 2–3 minutes, or until the eggs set.

7 Transfer the mixture to 4 warmed serving bowls and serve immediately.

SERVES 4

250 g/9 oz egg noodles
450 g/1 lb chicken thighs
2 tbsp groundnut oil
100 g/3½ oz carrots, sliced
3 tbsp oyster sauce
2 eggs
3 tbsp cold water

NUTRITION
Calories *278*; Sugars *2 g*; Protein *30 g*;
Carbohydrate *13 g*; Fat *12 g*; Saturates *3 g*

  easy

5 mins

25 mins

🍳 **COOK'S TIP**

Flavour the eggs with either soy sauce or hoisin sauce as an alternative to the oyster sauce, if you prefer.

One of those easy, delicious meals where the rice and fish are cooked together in one pan. Make sure the whole spices are removed before serving.

Aromatic Seafood Rice

SERVES 4

225 g/8 oz basmati rice
2 tbsp ghee or vegetable oil
1 onion, chopped
1 garlic clove, crushed
1 tsp cumin seeds
½–1 tsp chilli powder
4 cloves
1 cinnamon stick or a piece of cassia bark
2 tsp curry paste
225 g/8 oz peeled prawns
500g/1 lb 2 oz white fish fillets (such as monkfish, cod or haddock), skinned, boned and cut into bite-sized pieces
600 ml/1 pint boiling water
55 g/2 oz frozen peas
55 g/2 oz frozen sweetcorn kernels
1–2 tbsp lime juice
2 tbsp toasted desiccated coconut
salt and pepper

to garnish
1 fresh coriander sprig
2 lime slices

NUTRITION

Calories *380*; Sugars *2 g*; Protein *40 g*;
Carbohydrate *26 g*; Fat *13 g*; Saturates *5 g*

moderate

20 mins

25 mins

1 Place the rice in a sieve and wash well under cold running water until the water runs clear. Drain well.

2 Heat the ghee or vegetable oil in a large saucepan over a low heat. Add the onion, garlic, spices and curry paste and fry very gently for 1 minute.

3 Stir in the rice and mix well until coated in the spiced oil. Add the prawns and white fish. Season well with salt and pepper. Stir lightly, then pour in the boiling water.

4 Cover and cook gently for 10 minutes. Add the peas and sweetcorn, cover and cook for a further 8 minutes. Remove from the heat and leave to stand for 10 minutes.

5 Uncover the pan, fluff up the rice with a fork and transfer to a large warmed serving platter.

6 Sprinkle the dish with the lime juice and toasted coconut and garnish with a coriander sprig and 2 lime slices. Serve immediately.

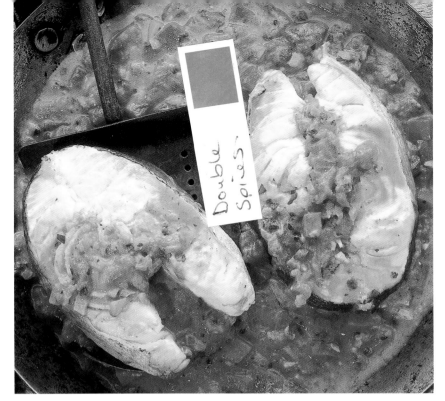

Quick and easy – cod steaks are cooked in a rich tomato and coconut sauce to produce tender, succulent results.

Indian Cod *with* Tomatoes

1 Heat the vegetable oil in a frying pan over a medium heat. Add the fish steaks and season to taste with salt and pepper. Fry until browned on both sides, but not cooked through. Remove from the pan and reserve.

2 Add the onion, garlic, red pepper and spices and cook very gently for about 2 minutes, stirring frequently. Add the tomatoes, bring to the boil and simmer for 5 minutes.

3 Add the fish steaks to the pan and simmer gently for 8 minutes, or until the fish is cooked through.

4 Remove the fish from the pan and keep warm in a serving dish. Add the coconut milk and coriander to the pan and reheat gently.

5 Spoon the sauce over the fish and serve immediately.

SERVES 4

3 tbsp vegetable oil
4 cod steaks, about 2.5-cm/1-inch thick
1 onion, chopped finely
2 garlic cloves, crushed
1 red pepper, deseeded and chopped
1 tsp ground coriander
1 tsp ground cumin
1 tsp ground turmeric
½ tsp garam masala
400 g/14 oz canned chopped tomatoes
150 ml/5 fl oz coconut milk
1–2 tbsp chopped fresh coriander or parsley
salt and pepper

NUTRITION
Calories *194*; Sugars *6 g*; Protein *21 g*;
Carbohydrate *7 g*; Fat *9 g*; Saturates *1 g*

⭐⭐   easy
🕐   5 mins
🕐   25 mins

 COOK'S TIP

The mixture may be flavoured with 1 tablespoon of curry powder or curry paste (mild, medium or hot, according to personal preference) instead of the mixture of spices in step 2, if you wish.

The moist texture of grilled plaice is complemented by the texture of the fresh mushrooms.

Plaice *with* Mushrooms

SERVES 4

4 white-skinned plaice fillets, about 150 g/5½ oz each
2 tbsp lime juice
85 g/3 oz low-fat spread
300 g/10½ oz mixed small mushrooms such as button, oyster, shiitake, chanterelle or morel, sliced or quartered
4 tomatoes, peeled, deseeded and chopped
celery salt and pepper
fresh basil leaves, to garnish
mixed salad, to serve

1 Line a grill rack with baking paper and place the fish on top.

2 Sprinkle over the lime juice and season to taste with celery salt and pepper.

3 Place under a preheated medium-hot grill and cook for 7–8 minutes without turning, until just cooked. Keep warm.

4 Meanwhile, gently melt the low fat spread in a non-stick frying pan over a low heat. Add the mushrooms and fry gently for 4–5 minutes, or until cooked through.

5 Gently heat the tomatoes in a small saucepan over a low heat.

6 Transfer the fish to 4 large serving plates and spoon over the mushrooms, with any pan juices, and the tomatoes. Garnish with a few basil leaves and serve with a mixed salad.

NUTRITION
Calories 243; Sugars 2 g; Protein 30 g;
Carbohydrate 2 g; Fat 13 g; Saturates 3 g

easy

10 mins

20 mins

 COOK'S TIP

Mushrooms are ideal in a low-fat diet, as they are packed full of flavour and contain no fat. More 'meaty' types of mushroom, such as chestnut, will take slightly longer to cook.

The firm, sweet flesh of the fresh trout is enhanced by the spicy flavour of the marinade.

Delicately Spiced Trout

1 Using a sharp knife, slash the trout skin in several places on both sides.

2 To make the marinade, mix all the ingredients together in a bowl.

3 Place the trout in a large, shallow dish and pour the marinade over. Cover and leave to marinate in the refrigerator for about 30–40 minutes, turning the fish occasionally.

4 Heat the sunflower oil in a preheated wok or Balti pan over a medium heat. Add the fennel seeds and onion seeds and fry until they start popping.

5 Add the garlic, coconut milk and tomato purée and bring the mixture to the boil.

6 Add the sultanas, garam masala and trout with the juices from the marinade. Cover and simmer for 5 minutes. Turn the trout over carefully and simmer for a further 10 minutes.

7 Transfer the trout to 4 warmed serving plates, garnish with cashew nuts, lemon and coriander sprigs. Serve immediately.

SERVES 4

4 trout, about 175–250 g/6–9 oz
    each, cleaned
3 tbsp sunflower oil
1 tsp fennel seeds
1 tsp onion seeds
1 garlic clove, crushed
150 ml/5 fl oz coconut milk or fish stock
3 tbsp tomato purée
55 g/2 oz sultanas
½ tsp garam masala

marinade
4 tbsp lemon juice
2 tbsp chopped fresh coriander
1 tsp ground cumin
½ tsp salt
½ tsp ground black pepper

to garnish
25 g/1 oz cashew nuts, chopped
lemon wedges
4 fresh coriander sprigs

NUTRITION
Calories *374*; Sugars *13 g*; Protein *38 g*;
Carbohydrate *14 g*; Fat *19 g*; Saturates *3 g*

⭐⭐ easy

🕐 50 mins

🕐 20 mins

The combination of fresh and smoked fish gives these kebabs a very special flavour. Try to choose thick fish fillets for good, bite-sized chunks.

Smoky Fish Skewers

SERVES 4

350 g/12 oz smoked cod fillet
350 g/12 oz cod fillet
8 large raw prawns
8 bay leaves
fresh dill sprigs, to garnish (optional)

marinade

4 tbsp sunflower oil, plus a little
   for brushing
2 tbsp lemon or lime juice
grated rind of ½ lemon or lime
¼ tsp dried dill
salt and pepper

1 Skin both types of cod and cut the flesh into bite-sized pieces. Peel the prawns, leaving the tails intact.

2 To make the marinade, mix the sunflower oil, lemon or lime juice and rind, dried dill and seasoning together in a shallow, non-metallic dish.

3 Place the prepared fish in the marinade and stir well until the fish is coated on all sides. Cover and leave to marinate in the refrigerator for 1–4 hours.

4 Thread the fish on to 4 metal skewers, alternating the fish with the prawns and bay leaves.

5 Cover the barbecue rack with lightly oiled tinfoil. Place the fish skewers on top and cook on the barbecue over hot coals for 5–10 minutes, basting with any remaining marinade. Turn once.

6 Transfer the skewers to a warmed serving plate, garnish with fresh dill, if you wish and serve immediately.

NUTRITION

Calories *221*; Sugars *0 g*; Protein *33 g*;
Carbohydrate *0 g*; Fat *10 g*; Saturates *1 g*

 easy

 10 mins, plus 1–4 hrs

5–10 mins

COOK'S TIP

Cod fillet can be rather flaky, so choose the thicker end, which is easier to cut into chunky pieces. Cook the fish on tinfoil rather than directly on the rack, so that if the fish breaks away from the skewer, it is not wasted.

Since the scallops are marinated, it is not essential that they are live; thawed frozen shellfish will work well in this recipe.

Scallop Skewers

1 If using wooden skewers, soak 8 of them in cold water for at least 30 minutes before you use them. This prevents the skewers burning on the barbecue.

2 Mix the lime zest and juice, lemon grass, garlic and chilli together in a mortar with a pestle to make a paste. Alternatively, use a spice grinder.

3 Thread 2 scallops on to each of the presoaked skewers. Cover the ends with a piece of tinfoil to prevent them burning.

4 Alternate the scallops with the lime segments.

5 Place the sunflower oil and lemon juice in a small bowl. Season to taste with salt and pepper and whisk together to make a dressing.

6 Coat the scallops with the prepared spice paste and cook for 10 minutes over a medium-hot barbecue, basting occasionally. Turn the skewers once.

7 Toss the rocket, mixed salad leaves and dressing together and transfer to a serving bowl and garnish with fresh chives.

8 Serve the scallops piping hot, 2 skewers on each plate, with the salad.

SERVES 4

grated zest and juice of 2 limes
2 tbsp finely chopped lemon grass or 1 tbsp lemon juice
2 garlic cloves, crushed
1 fresh green chilli, deseeded and chopped
16 scallops, with corals
2 limes, each cut into 8 segments
2 tbsp sunflower oil
1 tbsp lemon juice
salt and pepper
fresh chives, to garnish

to serve

55 g/2 oz rocket salad
200 g/7 oz mixed salad leaves

NUTRITION

Calories *182*; Sugars *0 g*; Protein *29 g*; Carbohydrate *0 g*; Fat *7 g*; Saturates *1 g*

easy
30 mins
10 mins

Meat Dishes

Many of the meat dishes on offer may be classic and traditional, but they are all speedy to make, and use ingredients that can be store cupboard staples. Others have a modern twist but are equally simple to prepare.

The dishes in this chapter range from easy, economic midweek suppers to quick but sophisticated and elegant main courses for special occasions. All of the recipes are extremely wholesome, offering a comprehensive range of tastes. Those on a low-fat diet should use lean cuts of meat and look out for low-fat mince to enjoy the dishes featured here.

This quick and easy dish tastes superb and would make a delicious treat for a special occasion.

Creamed Strips *of* Sirloin

SERVES 4

6 tbsp butter
450 g/1 lb sirloin steak, trimmed and cut into thin strips
175 g/6 oz button mushrooms, sliced
1 tsp mustard
pinch of grated fresh root ginger
2 tbsp dry sherry
150 ml/5 fl oz double cream
salt and pepper
4 slices hot toast, cut into triangles, to serve

pasta
450 g/1 lb dried rigatoni
2 tsp olive oil
2 fresh basil sprigs
115 g/4 oz butter

NUTRITION
Calories *796*; Sugars *2 g*; Protein *29 g*;
Carbohydrate *26 g*; Fat *63 g*; Saturates *39 g*

easy

15 mins

30 mins

1 Melt the butter in a large frying pan over a low heat. Add the steak and fry, stirring frequently, for 6 minutes. Using a slotted spoon, transfer the steak to an ovenproof dish and keep warm.

2 Add the mushrooms to the frying pan and cook for 2–3 minutes in the juices remaining in the pan. Add the mustard and ginger and season to taste with salt and pepper. Cook for 2 minutes, then add the sherry and cream. Cook for a further 3 minutes, then pour the cream sauce over the steak.

3 Bake the steak and cream sauce in a preheated oven at 190°C/375°F/Gas Mark 5, for 10 minutes.

4 Meanwhile, bring a large saucepan of lightly salted water to the boil over a medium heat. Add the pasta, olive oil, 1 of the basil sprigs and cook for about 8–10 minutes, or until tender, but still firm to the bite. Drain the pasta and transfer to a warmed serving dish. Toss the pasta with the butter and garnish with the other basil sprig.

5 Serve the steak with the pasta and triangles of hot toast.

COOK'S TIP

Dried pasta will keep for up to 6 months. Keep it in the packet and reseal it once you have opened it, or transfer the pasta to an airtight jar.

Any variety of long pasta, such as tagliatelle or fettuccine, could be used for this very tasty dish from Sicily.

Sicilian Spaghetti Cake

1 Brush a 20-cm/8-inch loose-based round cake tin with a little olive oil, then line the base with oiled baking paper. Cut the aubergines into slanting slices 5-mm/¼-inch thick. Heat a little of the olive oil in a frying pan over a medium heat. Add a few slices of aubergine at a time and fry until lightly browned on both sides. Add more oil, as necessary. Drain on kitchen paper.

2 Put the beef, onion and garlic into a saucepan and dry-fry over a low heat, stirring frequently, until browned all over. Add the tomato purée, tomatoes, Worcestershire sauce and herbs. Season to taste with salt and pepper. Simmer gently for 10 minutes, stirring occasionally, then add the olives and pepper and cook for a further 10 minutes.

3 Bring a large saucepan of lightly salted water to the boil over a medium heat. Add the pasta and cook for 8–10 minutes, or until just tender, but still firm to the bite. Drain and transfer the pasta to a large bowl. Add the meat mixture and Parmesan cheese and toss together with 2 forks.

4 Arrange the aubergine in overlapping slices over the base and up the sides of the cake tin. Add the meat and cover with the remaining aubergine slices.

5 Stand the cake tin in a roasting tin and cook in a preheated oven at 200°C/400°F/Gas Mark 6, for 40 minutes. Remove from the oven, leave to stand in the tin for 5 minutes, then loosen around the edges and invert on to a warmed serving dish. Remove the baking paper and discard, then serve.

SERVES 4

150 ml/5 fl oz olive oil, plus extra for brushing
2 aubergines
350 g/12 oz lean beef mince
1 onion, chopped
2 garlic cloves, crushed
2 tbsp tomato purée
400 g/14 oz canned chopped tomatoes
1 tsp Worcestershire sauce
1 tsp chopped fresh oregano or marjoram or ½ tsp dried oregano or marjoram
40 g/1½ oz stoned black olives, sliced
1 green, red or yellow pepper, deseeded and chopped
175 g/6 oz dried spaghetti
125 g/4½ oz freshly grated Parmesan cheese
salt and pepper

NUTRITION
Calories *876*; Sugars *10 g*; Protein *37 g*; Carbohydrate *39 g*; Fat *65 g*; Saturates *18 g*

⭐⭐ easy
🕑 30 mins
🕐 50 mins

The combination of Italian and Indian ingredients makes a surprisingly delicious recipe. Marinate the steak in advance to save time and garnish with fresh coriander and flaked almonds, if you wish.

Beef *and* Pasta Bake

SERVES 4

900 g/2 lb steak, cut into cubes
150 ml/5 fl oz beef stock
450 g/1 lb dried macaroni
300 ml/10 fl oz double cream
½ tsp garam masala
salt
fresh coriander leaves, to garnish

korma paste

55 g/2 oz blanched almonds
6 garlic cloves
1½ tsp roughly chopped fresh root ginger
6 tbsp beef stock
1 tsp ground cardamom
4 cloves, crushed
1 tsp ground cinnamon
2 large onions, chopped
1 tsp coriander seeds
2 tsp ground cumin seeds
pinch of cayenne pepper
6 tbsp sunflower oil

NUTRITION

Calories *1050*; Sugars *4 g*; Protein *47 g*;
Carbohydrate *37 g*; Fat *81 g*; Saturates *34 g*

easy

6 hrs 15 mins

1 hr 15 mins

1 To make the korma paste, using a pestle and mortar grind the almonds finely. Put the ground almonds and the remaining korma paste ingredients into a food processor or blender and process to a very smooth paste.

2 Place the steak in a large, shallow dish and spoon over the korma paste, turning to coat the steak well. Leave to marinate in the refrigerator for at least 6 hours.

3 Transfer the steak and korma paste to a large saucepan and simmer over a low heat, adding a little beef stock, if required, for 35 minutes.

4 Meanwhile, bring a large saucepan of lightly salted water to the boil over a medium heat. Add the macaroni and cook for 8–10 minutes, or until tender, but still firm to the bite. Drain the macaroni thoroughly and transfer to a deep casserole. Add the steak, cream and garam masala.

5 Bake in a preheated oven at 200°C/ 400°F/Gas Mark 6, for 30 minutes, or until the steak is tender. Remove the casserole from the oven and leave to stand for about 10 minutes. Garnish the bake with fresh coriander and flaked almonds, if you wish and serve immediately.

A different twist is given to this traditional pasta dish with a rich, but subtle sauce.

Meatballs *in* Red Wine Sauce

1 Pour the milk into a bowl, add the breadcrumbs and soak for 30 minutes.

2 Heat half the butter and 4 tablespoons of the olive oil in a frying pan over a low heat. Add the mushrooms and fry for 4 minutes, then stir in the flour and cook for 2 minutes. Stir in the stock and wine and simmer for about 15 minutes. Add the tomatoes, tomato purée, sugar and basil. Season to taste with salt and pepper and simmer for 30 minutes.

3 Mix the shallots, steak and paprika with the breadcrumbs and season to taste. Shape the mixture into 14 meatballs.

4 Heat 4 tablespoons of the remaining olive oil and butter in a large frying pan over a medium heat. Add the meatballs and fry, turning frequently, until browned all over. Transfer to a deep casserole, pour over the sauce, cover and bake in a preheated oven at 180°C/350°F/Gas Mark 4, for 30 minutes.

5 Bring a large saucepan of lightly salted water to the boil over a medium heat. Add the pasta and remaining oil and cook for 8–10 minutes, or until tender, but still firm to the bite. Drain and transfer to a serving dish. Remove the casserole from the oven and leave to cool for 3 minutes, then pour the meatballs and sauce on to the pasta. Garnish with a basil sprig and serve.

SERVES 4

150 ml/5 fl oz milk
150 g/5½ oz white breadcrumbs
25 g/1 oz butter
9 tbsp olive oil
225 g/8 oz sliced oyster mushrooms
25 g/1 oz wholemeal flour
200 ml/7 fl oz beef stock
150 ml/5 fl oz red wine
4 tomatoes, peeled and chopped
1 tbsp tomato purée
1 tsp brown sugar
1 tbsp finely chopped fresh basil
12 shallots, chopped
450 g/1 lb lean steak mince
1 tsp paprika
450 g/1 lb dried egg tagliarini
salt and pepper
1 fresh basil sprig, to garnish

NUTRITION

Calories *811*; Sugars *7 g*; Protein *30 g*; Carbohydrate *76 g*; Fat *43 g*; Saturates *12 g*

 moderate

🕐 45 mins

🕐 1 hr 30 mins

The fresh taste of sage is the perfect ingredient to counteract the richness of the pork in this quick and simple dish.

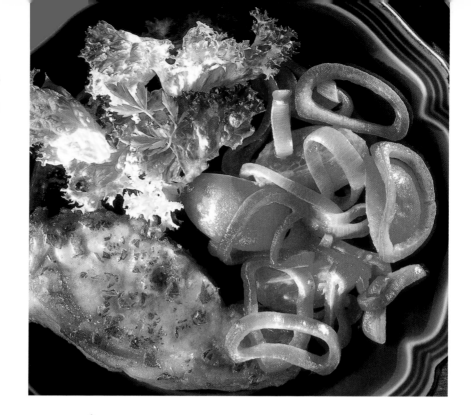

Pork Chops *with* Sage

SERVES 4

2 tbsp flour
1 tbsp chopped fresh sage or 1 tsp dried sage
4 boneless, lean pork chops, trimmed of excess fat
2 tbsp olive oil
15 g/½ oz butter
2 red onions, sliced into rings
1 tbsp lemon juice
2 tsp caster sugar
4 plum tomatoes, quartered
salt and pepper
green salad, to serve

1 Mix the flour, sage and salt and pepper to taste on a large plate. Lightly dust the pork chops on both sides with the seasoned flour.

2 Heat the olive oil and butter in a large frying pan over a medium heat. Add the pork chops and cook for 6–7 minutes on each side until cooked through. Drain the pork chops, reserving the pan juices and keep warm.

3 Toss the onion in the lemon juice and add to the pan. Fry with the sugar and tomatoes for 5 minutes until tender.

4 Transfer the pork chops to 4 warmed serving plates and pour over the pan juices. Serve with the tomato and onion mixture and a green salad.

NUTRITION
Calories 364; Sugars 5 g; Protein 34 g;
Carbohydrate 14 g; Fat 19 g; Saturates 7 g

easy

10 mins

15 mins

This unusual and attractive dish is extremely delicious. Make the Italian Red Wine Sauce (see page 15) well in advance to reduce the preparation time.

Pasta *and* Pork in Cream Sauce

1 Using a meat mallet or the end of a rolling pin, pound the slices of pork between 2 sheets of cling film until wafer thin, then cut into strips.

2 Heat the olive oil in a large frying pan over a medium heat. Add the pork and stir-fry for 5 minutes. Add the mushrooms and stir-fry for 2 minutes.

3 Pour over the Italian red wine sauce (see page 15), reduce the heat and simmer gently for 20 minutes.

4 Meanwhile, bring a large saucepan of lightly salted water to the boil over a medium heat. Add the lemon juice, saffron and pasta and cook for about 8–10 minutes, or until tender, but still firm to the bite. Drain thoroughly and keep warm.

5 Stir the cream into the pan with the pork and heat gently for a few minutes.

6 Bring a small saucepan of water to the boil over a medium heat. Add the eggs and boil for 3 minutes, then cool in cold water and remove the shells.

7 Transfer the pasta to a large, warmed serving plate, top with the pork and the sauce and garnish with the eggs. Serve immediately.

SERVES 4

450 g/1 lb pork fillet, sliced thinly
4 tbsp olive oil
225 g/8 oz button mushrooms, sliced
200 ml/7 fl oz Italian Red Wine Sauce (see page 15)
1 tbsp lemon juice
pinch of saffron
350 g/12 oz dried orecchioni
4 tbsp double cream
12 quail eggs (see Cook's Tip)
salt

NUTRITION
Calories 735; Sugars 4 g; Protein 31 g; Carbohydrate 37 g; Fat 52 g; Saturates 19 g

 moderate

 8 hrs 45 mins

35 mins

🍳 **COOK'S TIP**

In this recipe, the quail eggs are soft-boiled. As they are extremely difficult to shell when warm, it is important that they are thoroughly cooled first. Otherwise, they will break up unattractively.

The addition of juniper berries and fennel to the pork chops gives an unusual and delicate flavour to this dish.

Citrus Pork Chops

SERVES 4

½ fennel bulb
1 tbsp juniper berries, crushed lightly
about 2 tbsp olive oil
finely grated rind of 1 orange
4 pork chops, about 150 g/5½ oz each
juice of 1 orange
crisp salad, to serve

1 Using a sharp knife, finely chop the fennel bulb. Discard the tough outer leaves and feathery fronds.

2 Grind the juniper berries in a mortar with a pestle. Mix the crushed juniper berries with the fennel flesh, olive oil and orange rind.

3 Using a sharp knife, score a few cuts over each pork chop.

4 Place the pork chops in a large roasting tin or an ovenproof dish, then spoon the fennel and juniper mixture over the pork chops.

5 Carefully pour the orange juice over the top of each pork chop, cover and leave to marinate in the refrigerator for about 2 hours.

6 Cook the pork chops, under a preheated hot grill, for 10–15 minutes, depending on the thickness of the meat, turning occasionally, until the meat is tender and cooked through.

7 Transfer the pork chops to 4 large, warmed serving plates and serve immediately with a crisp salad.

NUTRITION
Calories 274; Sugars 0 g; Protein 38.4 g;
Carbohydrate 0 g; Fat 13.9 g; Saturates 3 g

★★ easy
🕐 2 hrs 15 mins
🕐 10 –15 mins

 COOK'S TIP

Juniper berries are most commonly associated with gin, but they are often added to meat dishes in Italy for a delicate citrus flavour. They can be bought dried from most health food shops and all supermarkets.

This is a simplified version of a traditional dish from the Marche region of Italy. Pork fillet pockets are stuffed with Parma ham and fresh oregano.

Pork *with* Lemon *and* Garlic

1 Using a sharp knife, cut the pork fillet into 4 equal pieces. Place the pork between 2 sheets of greaseproof paper and pound each piece with a meat mallet or the end of a rolling pin to flatten.

2 Cut a horizontal slit in each piece of pork to make a pocket.

3 Place the almonds on a baking tray and lightly toast under a preheated medium-hot grill for 2–3 minutes, or until golden.

4 Mix the almonds with 1 tablespoon of olive oil, Parma ham, garlic, oregano and the finely grated rind from 1 lemon. Spoon the mixture into the pockets of the pork.

5 Heat the remaining olive oil in a large frying pan over a medium heat. Add the shallots and cook for 2 minutes.

6 Add the pork to the frying pan and cook for 2 minutes on each side, or until browned all over.

7 Add the ham or chicken stock to the pan, bring to the boil over a medium heat. Cover and simmer for 45 minutes, or until the pork is tender. Remove the pork from the pan, reserve and keep warm.

8 Add the remaining lemon rind and sugar to the pan, then boil for about 3–4 minutes, or until reduced and syrupy. Transfer the pork to 4 warmed serving plates and pour over the sauce. Serve with sugar snap peas.

SERVES 4

450 g/1 lb pork fillet
50 g/1¾ oz chopped almonds
2 tbsp olive oil
100 g/3½ oz Parma ham, chopped finely
2 garlic cloves, chopped
1 tbsp fresh oregano, chopped
finely grated rind of 2 lemons
4 shallots, chopped finely
200 ml/7 fl oz ham or chicken stock
1 tsp sugar
freshly cooked sugar snap peas, to serve

NUTRITION
Calories *428*; Sugars *2 g*; Protein *31 g*;
Carbohydrate *4 g*; Fat *32 g*; Saturates *4 g*

easy

25 mins

 1 hr

Chunks of tender lamb, pan-fried with garlic and stewed in red wine is a traditional Roman dish.

Lamb *and* Anchovies *with* Thyme

SERVES 4

1 tbsp olive oil
15 g/½ oz butter
600 g/1 lb 5 oz lamb (shoulder or leg), cut in 2.5-cm/1-inch chunks
4 garlic cloves
3 fresh thyme sprigs, stalks removed
6 canned anchovy fillets
150 ml/5 fl oz red wine
150 ml/5 fl oz lamb or vegetable stock
1 tsp sugar
50 g/1¾ oz stoned black olives, halved
2 tbsp chopped fresh parsley, to garnish

1 Heat the olive oil and butter in a frying pan over a medium heat. Add the lamb and cook for 4–5 minutes, stirring, until the meat is browned all over.

2 Grind the garlic, thyme and anchovies together in a mortar with a pestle to make a smooth paste.

3 Add the wine and lamb stock to the frying pan. Stir in the garlic and anchovy paste together with the sugar.

4 Bring the mixture to the boil over a medium heat, then reduce the heat, cover and simmer for 30–40 minutes, or until the lamb is tender. For the last 10 minutes of cooking, remove the lid to allow the sauce to reduce slightly.

5 Stir the olives into the sauce and mix well.

6 Transfer the lamb and sauce to a large, warmed serving bowl and garnish with chopped parsley. Serve immediately.

NUTRITION

Calories *299*; Sugars *1 g*; Protein *31 g*; Carbohydrate *1 g*; Fat *16 g*; Saturates *7 g*

 moderate

 15 mins

15 mins

50 mins

A classic combination of flavours, this dish would make a perfect Sunday lunch. Serve with tomato and onion salad and jacket baked potatoes.

Lamb Cutlets *with* Rosemary

1 Trim the lamb cutlets by cutting away the flesh with a sharp knife to expose the tips of the bones.

2 Place the oil, lemon juice, garlic, lemon pepper and salt in a large, shallow, non-metallic dish and mix with a fork.

3 Lay the rosemary sprigs in the dish and place the lamb on top. Cover and leave to marinate in the refrigerator for at least 1 hour, turning the lamb cutlets once.

4 Remove the lamb cutlets from the marinade and wrap a piece of tinfoil around the bones to stop them burning on the barbecue.

5 Place the rosemary sprigs on a barbecue rack and place the lamb on top. Cook on a hot barbecue over hot coals for 10–15 minutes, turning once.

6 Meanwhile, make the salad and dressing. Arrange the tomatoes on a serving dish and scatter the spring onions on top. Place all the ingredients for the dressing in a screw-top jar, shake well and pour over the salad. Serve with the barbecued lamb cutlets and jacket baked potatoes.

SERVES 4

8 lamb cutlets
5 tbsp olive oil
2 tbsp lemon juice
1 garlic clove, crushed
½ tsp lemon pepper
salt
8 fresh rosemary sprigs
jacket baked potatoes, to serve

salad
4 tomatoes, sliced
4 spring onions, sliced diagonally

dressing
2 tbsp olive oil
1 tbsp lemon juice
1 garlic clove, chopped
¼ tsp chopped fresh rosemary

NUTRITION
Calories *560*; Sugars *1 g*; Protein *48 g*; Carbohydrate *1 g*; Fat *40 g*; Saturates *1 g*

 moderate

 1 hr 15 mins

15 mins

🍲 **COOK'S TIP**

Choose medium to small baking potatoes if you want to cook jacket baked potatoes on the barbecue. Scrub them well, prick with a fork and wrap in buttered tinfoil. Bury them in the hot coals and barbecue for 50–60 minutes.

These lamb chops quickly become more elegant when the bone is removed to make noisettes.

Lamb *with* Bay *and* Lemon

SERVES 4

4 lamb chops
1 tbsp olive oil
15 g/½ oz butter
150 ml/5 fl oz white wine
150 ml/5 fl oz lamb or vegetable stock
2 bay leaves
pared rind of 1 lemon
salt and pepper

1 Using a sharp knife, carefully remove the bone from each lamb chop, keeping the meat intact. Alternatively, ask the butcher to prepare the lamb noisettes for you.

2 Shape the meat into rounds and secure with a length of string.

3 Heat the olive oil and butter together in a frying pan over a medium heat until the mixture starts to froth.

4 Add the lamb noisettes to the frying pan and cook for 2–3 minutes on each side, or until the meat is browned all over.

5 Remove the pan from the heat, drain off all of the excess fat and discard.

6 Return the frying pan to the heat. Add the wine, stock, bay leaves and lemon rind to the frying pan and cook for 20–25 minutes, or until the lamb is tender. Season the lamb noisettes and sauce to taste with salt and pepper.

7 Transfer to 4 large, warmed serving plates. Remove the string from each noisette, discard the bay leaves and serve with the sauce.

NUTRITION

Calories *268*; Sugars *0.2 g*; Protein *24 g*;
Carbohydrate *0.2 g*; Fat *16 g*; Saturates *7 g*

  moderate

🕙 10 mins

🕐 35 mins

The appearance of the leg of lamb as it is opened out to cook on the barbecue gives this dish its name.

Butterfly Lamb *with* Mint

1 Open out the boned leg of lamb so its shape resembles a butterfly, then thread 2–3 metal skewers through the meat to make it easier to turn on the barbecue.

2 Mix the balsamic vinegar, lemon rind and juice, sunflower oil, chopped mint, garlic and sugar together in a non-metallic dish large enough to hold the lamb. Season to taste with salt and pepper.

3 Place the lamb in the dish and turn until it is coated on both sides with the marinade. Cover and leave to marinate in the refrigerator for at least 6 hours, or preferably overnight, turning occasionally.

4 Remove the lamb from the marinade and reserve the liquid for basting.

5 Place the barbecue rack about 15 cm/6 inches above the coals on a hot barbecue and cook the lamb for about 30 minutes on each side, turning once and basting frequently with the marinade.

6 Transfer the lamb to a chopping board and remove the skewers. Cut the lamb into slices across the grain and transfer to 4 warmed serving plates. Serve with grilled vegetables with olives and salad leaves.

SERVES 4

boned leg of lamb, about 1.8 kg/4 lb
8 tbsp balsamic vinegar
grated rind and juice of 1 lemon
150 ml/5 fl oz sunflower oil
4 tbsp chopped fresh mint
2 garlic cloves, crushed
2 tbsp light muscovado sugar
salt and pepper

to serve
grilled vegetables with olives
green salad leaves

NUTRITION
Calories *733*; Sugars *6 g*; Protein *69 g*;
Carbohydrate *6 g*; Fat *48 g*; Saturates *13 g*

easy

10 mins, plus 6 hrs

1 hr

This truly spectacular dish is equally delicious whether you use veal or pork fillet. Make sure the roses are free of blemishes and pesticides.

Veal *in a* Rose Petal Sauce

SERVES 4

450 g/1 lb dried fettuccine
6 tbsp olive oil
1 tsp chopped fresh oregano
1 tsp chopped fresh marjoram
175 g/6 oz butter
450 g/1 lb veal fillet, sliced thinly
150 ml/5 fl oz rose petal vinegar (see Cook's Tip)
150 ml/5 fl oz fish stock
50 ml/2 fl oz grapefruit juice
50 ml/2 fl oz double cream
salt

to garnish
12 pink grapefruit segments
12 pink peppercorns
rose petals, washed
fresh herb leaves

1 Bring a large saucepan of lightly salted water to the boil over a medium heat. Add the pasta and cook for 8–10 minutes, or until tender, but still firm to the bite. Drain and transfer to a warmed serving dish, sprinkle over 2 tablespoons of the olive oil, the oregano and marjoram.

2 Heat 55 g/2 oz of the butter with the remaining olive oil in a large frying pan over a low heat. Add the veal and cook for 6 minutes. Remove the veal from the pan and place on top of the pasta. Keep warm.

3 Add the vinegar and fish stock to the pan and bring to the boil over a medium heat. Boil vigorously until reduced by two thirds. Add the grapefruit juice and cream, reduce the heat and simmer for 4 minutes. Dice the remaining butter and add to the pan, a piece at a time, whisking constantly, until it has been incorporated.

4 Pour the sauce around the veal, garnish with grapefruit segments, pink peppercorns, rose petals and your favourite herb leaves. Serve.

NUTRITION
Calories *475*; Sugars *3.6 g*; Protein *39 g*;
Carbohydrate *104 g*; Fat *52 g*; Saturates *16 g*

easy

20 mins

25 mins

🍽 **COOK'S TIP**

To make the rose petal vinegar, infuse the petals of 8 pesticide-free roses in 150 ml/5 fl oz white wine vinegar for 48 hours. Prepare well in advance to reduce the preparation time.

The delicious combination of apple, onion and mushroom perfectly complements the delicate flavour of the veal.

Neapolitan Veal Cutlets

1 Melt 55 g/2 oz of the butter in a frying pan over a low heat. Add the veal and fry for 5 minutes on each side. Transfer to a dish and keep warm.

2 Add the onion and apples to the pan and fry over a low heat until lightly browned. Transfer to a dish, place the veal on top and keep warm.

3 Melt the remaining butter in the frying pan over a low heat. Add the mushrooms, tarragon and peppercorns and fry gently for 3 minutes. Sprinkle over the sesame seeds.

4 Bring a large saucepan of lightly salted water to the boil over a medium heat. Add the pasta and 1 teaspoon of the olive oil and cook for about 8–10 minutes, or until tender, but still firm to the bite. Drain well and transfer to an ovenproof serving dish.

5 Cook the tomatoes and basil leaves under a preheated hot grill for 2–3 minutes. Dot the pasta with the mascarpone and sprinkle with the remaining olive oil. Place the onions, apples and veal on top, then spoon the mushrooms and peppercorns over with the pan juices. Season to taste with salt and pepper. Place the tomatoes and basil around the edge and cook in a preheated oven at 150°C/300°F/Gas Mark 2, for 5 minutes.

6 Transfer to 4 serving plates and serve immediately.

SERVES 4

200 g/7 oz butter
4 veal cutlets, about 250 g/9 oz each, trimmed
1 large onion, sliced
2 apples, peeled, cored and sliced
175 g/6 oz button mushrooms
1 tbsp chopped fresh tarragon
8 black peppercorns
1 tbsp sesame seeds
400 g/14 oz dried marille pasta
100 ml/3½ fl oz extra virgin olive oil
2 large beef tomatoes, cut in half
leaves of 1 fresh basil sprig
175 g/6 oz mascarpone cheese
salt and pepper

NUTRITION
Calories 1071; Sugars 13 g; Protein 74 g; Carbohydrate 66 g; Fat 59 g; Saturates 16 g

✪✪✪✪ challenging

🕐 20 mins

🕐 45 mins

This dish is really superb if made with tender veal. However, if veal is unavailable, use pork or turkey escalopes instead.

Veal Italienne

SERVES 4

55 g/2 oz butter
1 tbsp olive oil
650 g/1 lb 7 oz potatoes, peeled and cubed
4 veal escalopes, 175 g/6 oz each
1 onion, cut into 8 wedges
2 garlic cloves, crushed
2 tbsp plain flour
2 tbsp tomato purée
150 ml/5 fl oz red wine
300 ml/10 fl oz chicken stock
8 ripe tomatoes, peeled, deseeded and diced
25 g/1 oz stoned black olives, halved
2 tbsp chopped fresh basil
salt and pepper
fresh basil leaves, to garnish

1 Heat the butter and oil in a large non-stick frying pan over a medium heat. Add the potato cubes and cook for 5–7 minutes, stirring frequently, until they start to brown.

2 Remove the potatoes from the pan with a slotted spoon and reserve.

3 Place the veal in the frying pan and cook for 2–3 minutes on each side until sealed. Remove from the pan and reserve.

4 Add the onion and garlic to the frying pan and cook for 2–3 minutes.

5 Add the flour and tomato purée and cook for 1 minute, stirring. Gradually blend in the red wine and chicken stock, stirring constantly, to make a smooth sauce.

6 Return the potatoes and veal to the pan. Stir in the tomatoes, olives and chopped basil and season to taste with salt and pepper.

7 Transfer to a casserole and cook in a preheated oven at 180°C/350°F/Gas Mark 4, for 1 hour, or until the potatoes and veal are cooked through. Transfer to 4 warmed serving plates, garnish with basil leaves and serve.

NUTRITION

Calories 592; Sugars 5 g; Protein 44 g; Carbohydrate 48 g; Fat 23 g; Saturates 9 g

moderate

25 mins

1 hr 20 mins

🍳 COOK'S TIP

For a quicker cooking time and really tender meat, place the meat between 2 sheets of greaseproof paper and pound with a meat mallet or the end of a rolling pin to flatten it slightly before cooking.

Anchovies are often used to enhance flavour, particularly in meat dishes. Either veal or turkey escalopes can be used for this pan-fried dish.

Escalopes *and* Italian Sausage

1 Heat the olive oil in a large frying pan over a medium heat. Add the anchovy fillets, capers, fresh rosemary, orange rind and juice, Italian sausage and tomatoes and cook for 5–6 minutes, stirring occasionally.

2 Meanwhile, place the veal or turkey escalopes between 2 sheets of greaseproof paper and pound with a meat mallet or the end of a rolling pin to flatten slightly.

3 Add the meat to the mixture in the frying pan. Season to taste with salt and pepper, cover and cook for 3–5 minutes on each side, slightly longer if the meat is thicker.

4 Transfer to 4 warmed serving plates and serve with cooked polenta.

SERVES 4

1 tbsp olive oil
6 canned anchovy fillets, drained
1 tbsp capers, drained
1 tbsp fresh rosemary, stalks removed
finely grated rind and juice of 1 orange
75 g/2¾ oz Italian sausage, diced
3 tomatoes, peeled and chopped
4 veal or turkey escalopes, about
    125 g/4½ oz each
salt and pepper
cooked polenta, to serve

NUTRITION
Calories *233*; Sugars *1 g*; Protein *28 g*;
Carbohydrate *1 g*; Fat *13 g*; Saturates *1 g*

 easy

🕐 10 mins

🕐 20 mins

🍳 **COOK'S TIP**

Try using 4-minute steaks, slightly flattened, instead of the turkey or veal. Cook them for 4–5 minutes on top of the sauce in the pan.

Poultry

For the poultry-lover there are pasta dishes, roasts and bakes in this chapter, incorporating a variety of healthy and colourful ingredients. For those who enjoy Italian cuisine, there are a number of rich Italian sauces and old favourites including more traditional casseroles, such as Rich Chicken Casserole and Chicken Cacciatora. All of these recipes are mouthwatering and quick and easy to prepare. They are also extremely wholesome, offering a comprehensive range of tastes.

There is a delicious surprise of creamy herb and garlic soft cheese hidden inside these chicken parcels!

Garlic *and* Herb Chicken

SERVES 4

4 chicken breasts, skinned
100 g/3½ oz full fat soft cheese, flavoured
 with herbs and garlic
8 slices Parma ham
150 ml/5 fl oz red wine
150 ml/5 fl oz chicken stock
1 tbsp brown sugar
green salad leaves, to serve

1 Using a sharp knife, make a horizontal slit along the length of each chicken breast to form a pocket.

2 Place the cheese in a small bowl and beat with a wooden spoon to soften it. Spoon the cheese into the pocket of the chicken breasts.

3 Wrap 2 slices of Parma ham around each chicken breast and secure firmly in place with a length of string.

4 Pour the wine and chicken stock into a large frying pan and bring to the boil over a medium heat. When the mixture is just starting to boil, add the sugar and stir to dissolve.

5 Add the chicken breasts to the mixture in the frying pan. Simmer for about 12–15 minutes, or until the chicken is tender and the juices run clear when a skewer is inserted into the thickest part of the meat.

6 Remove the chicken from the pan, reserve and keep warm.

7 Reheat the sauce and boil until reduced and thickened. Remove the string from the chicken and cut into slices. Pour the sauce over the chicken and serve with salad leaves.

NUTRITION
Calories 272; Sugars 4 g; Protein 29 g;
Carbohydrate 4 g; Fat 13 g; Saturates 6 g

easy

30 mins

25 mins

(🍳) **COOK'S TIP**

Try adding 2 finely chopped sun-dried tomatoes to the soft cheese in step 2, if you prefer.

This casserole is packed with the sunshine flavours of Italy. The sun-dried tomatoes add a wonderful richness to the dish.

Rich Chicken Casserole

1 Place the chicken in a large heavy-based frying pan and fry without fat over a fairly high heat, turning occasionally, until golden brown. Using a slotted spoon, drain off any excess fat from the chicken and transfer to a large flameproof casserole dish.

2 Heat the olive oil in the pan over a medium heat. Add the onion, garlic and pepper and fry for 3–4 minutes. Transfer the vegetables to the casserole.

3 Add the orange rind and juice, chicken stock, chopped tomatoes and sun-dried tomatoes to the casserole and mix well.

4 Bring to the boil, then cover the casserole with a lid and simmer very gently over a low heat for about 1 hour, stirring occasionally. Add the chopped fresh thyme and black olives, then season to taste with salt and pepper.

5 Spoon the chicken casserole on to 4 warmed serving plates, garnish with orange rind and thyme sprigs and serve with crusty bread.

SERVES 4

8 chicken thighs
2 tbsp olive oil
1 medium red onion, sliced
2 garlic cloves, crushed
1 large red pepper, sliced thickly
thinly pared rind and juice of 1 small orange
125 ml/4 fl oz chicken stock
400 g/14 oz canned chopped tomatoes
25 g/1 oz sun-dried tomatoes, sliced thinly
1 tbsp chopped fresh thyme
50 g/1¾ oz stoned black olives
salt and pepper
crusty bread, to serve

to garnish
orange rind
4 fresh thyme sprigs

NUTRITION
Calories *320*; Sugars *8 g*; Protein *34 g*;
Carbohydrate *8 g*; Fat *17 g*; Saturates *4 g*

 moderate

 15 mins

15 mins

1 hr 15 mins

👨‍🍳 **COOK'S TIP**

Sun-dried tomatoes have a dense texture and concentrated taste and add intense flavour to slow-cooking casseroles.

Fresh spinach ribbon noodles, topped with a rich tomato sauce and creamy chicken, make a very appetising dish.

Pasta *with* Chicken Sauce

SERVES 4

250 g/9 oz fresh green tagliatelle
1 tsp olive oil
fresh basil leaves, to garnish
salt and pepper

tomato sauce

2 tbsp olive oil
1 small onion, chopped
1 garlic clove, chopped
400 g/14 oz canned chopped tomatoes
2 tbsp chopped fresh parsley
1 tsp dried oregano
2 bay leaves
2 tbsp tomato purée
1 tsp sugar

chicken sauce

4 tbsp unsalted butter
400 g/14 oz boned chicken breasts,
    skinned and cut into thin strips
85 g/3 oz blanched almonds
300 ml/10 fl oz double cream

NUTRITION

Calories *995*; Sugars *8 g*; Protein *36 g*;
Carbohydrate *50 g*; Fat *74 g*; Saturates *34 g*

  moderate

🕐 15 mins

🕐 45 mins

1 To make the tomato sauce, heat the olive oil in a saucepan over a medium heat. Add the onion and fry until translucent. Add the garlic and fry for 1 minute. Stir in the chopped tomatoes, parsley, oregano, bay leaves, tomato purée and sugar. Season to taste with salt and pepper, bring to the boil and simmer, uncovered, for 15–20 minutes, until reduced by half. Remove the saucepan from the heat and discard the bay leaves.

2 To make the chicken sauce, gently melt the butter in a frying pan over a medium heat. Add the chicken and almonds and stir-fry for 5–6 minutes, or until the chicken is cooked through.

3 Meanwhile, bring the cream to the boil in a small saucepan over a low heat and boil for about 10 minutes, until reduced by almost half. Pour the cream over the chicken and almonds, stir and season to taste with salt and pepper. Reserve and keep warm.

4 Bring a large saucepan of lightly salted water to the boil over a medium heat. Add the pasta and olive oil and cook for 8–10 minutes, or until tender, but still firm to the bite. Drain and transfer to a warmed serving dish. Spoon over the tomato sauce and arrange the chicken sauce down the centre. Garnish with a few basil leaves and serve immediately.

All the warm colours and flavours of the Mediterranean are combined in this easy dish.

Chicken Pepperonata

1 Remove the skin from the chicken thighs and toss in the flour.

2 Heat the oil in a wide frying pan over a high heat. Add the chicken and quickly fry until sealed and lightly browned, then remove from the pan. Add the onion to the pan and fry until soft. Add the garlic, peppers, tomatoes and oregano, then bring to the boil, stirring constantly.

3 Arrange the chicken over the vegetables, season well with salt and pepper. Cover the pan tightly and simmer for 20–25 minutes, or until the chicken is tender and the juices run clear when a skewer is inserted into the thickest part of the meat.

4 Season to taste, then transfer the chicken to a large serving dish. Garnish with oregano leaves and serve.

SERVES 4

8 skinless chicken thighs
2 tbsp wholemeal flour
2 tbsp olive oil
1 small onion, sliced thinly
1 garlic clove, crushed
1 each large red, yellow and green peppers, sliced thinly
400 g/14 oz canned chopped tomatoes
1 tbsp chopped oregano
salt and pepper
fresh oregano leaves, to garnish

NUTRITION
Calories *328*; Sugars *7 g*; Protein *35 g*; Carbohydrate *13 g*; Fat *15 g*; Saturates *4 g*

    easy
         15 mins
         40 mins

 COOK'S TIP

For extra flavour, halve the peppers and cook under a preheated hot grill until the skins are charred. Leave to cool, then remove the skins and seeds. Slice the peppers thinly and use in the recipe.

The refreshing combination of chicken and orange makes this a perfect dish for a warm summer evening.

Chicken *with* Orange Sauce

SERVES 4

30 ml/1 fl oz rapeseed oil

3 tbsp olive oil

4 skinless, boneless chicken breasts, about 225 g/8 oz each

150 ml/5 fl oz brandy

15 g/½ oz plain flour

150 ml/5 fl oz freshly squeezed orange juice

25 g/1 oz courgette, cut into matchsticks

25 g/1 oz red pepper, cut into matchsticks

25 g/1 oz leek, shredded finely

400 g/14 oz dried wholemeal spaghetti

3 large oranges, peeled and cut into segments

rind of 1 orange, cut into very fine strips

2 tbsp chopped fresh tarragon

150 ml/5 fl oz fromage frais or ricotta cheese

salt and pepper

NUTRITION

Calories 797; Sugars 28 g; Protein 59 g; Carbohydrate 77 g; Fat 25 g; Saturates 6 g

moderate

15 mins

25 mins

1 Heat the rapeseed oil and 1 tablespoon of the olive oil in a frying pan over a fairly high heat. Add the chicken and cook quickly until golden brown. Add the brandy and cook for 3 minutes. Sprinkle over the flour and cook, stirring constantly, for 2 minutes.

2 Reduce the heat and add the orange juice, courgette, pepper and leek. Season to taste with salt and pepper. Simmer for 5 minutes until the sauce has thickened.

3 Meanwhile, bring a large saucepan of lightly salted water to the boil over a medium heat. Add the pasta and cook for 10 minutes, or until tender, but still firm to the bite. Drain thoroughly, transfer to a serving dish and drizzle over the remaining olive oil.

4 Add half the orange segments, half the orange rind, the tarragon and fromage frais to the chicken in the pan and cook, stirring, for 3 minutes.

5 Place the chicken on top of the pasta, pour over a little orange sauce, garnish with the remaining orange segments and rind. Serve immediately with any extra sauce.

These unusual chicken kebabs have a wonderful Italian flavour, and the bacon helps keep them moist during cooking.

Skewered Chicken Spirals

1 Spread out a chicken breast between 2 sheets of clingfilm and beat firmly with a meat mallet or rolling pin to flatten the chicken to an even thickness. Repeat with the remaining chicken breasts.

2 Mix the garlic and tomato purée together and spread over the chicken. Lay a bacon slice over each, then sprinkle with the basil. Season to taste with salt and pepper.

3 Roll up each piece of chicken firmly, then cut into thick slices.

4 Thread the slices on to 4 metal skewers, making sure the skewer holds the chicken in a spiral shape.

5 Brush lightly with vegetable oil and cook over hot coals on a barbecue or under a preheated hot grill for about 10 minutes, turning once. Serve immediately with a green salad.

SERVES 4

4 skinless, boneless chicken breasts
1 garlic clove, crushed
2 tbsp tomato purée
4 slices smoked back bacon
large handful of fresh basil leaves
2 tbsp vegetable oil for brushing
salt and pepper
green salad, to serve

NUTRITION
Calories 231; Sugars 1 g; Protein 29 g;
Carbohydrate 1 g; Fat 13 g; Saturates 5 g

  easy

15 mins

10 mins

A rich caramelized sauce, flavoured with balsamic vinegar and wine, gives this chicken dish a piquant flavour.

Chicken *with* Balsamic Vinegar

SERVES 4

4 boneless chicken thighs
2 garlic cloves, crushed
200 ml/7 fl oz red wine
3 tbsp white wine vinegar
1 tbsp olive oil
15 g/½ oz butter
4 shallots
3 tbsp balsamic vinegar
2 tbsp fresh thyme
salt and pepper
cooked polenta or rice, to serve

1 Using a sharp knife, make a few slashes in the skin of the chicken. Brush the chicken with the crushed garlic and place in a large, shallow dish.

2 Pour the red wine and white wine vinegar over the chicken and season to taste with salt and pepper. Cover with clingfilm and leave to marinate in the refrigerator overnight.

3 Remove the chicken thighs with a slotted spoon, draining well, and reserve the marinade.

4 Heat the olive oil and butter in a large frying pan over a medium heat. Add the shallots and cook, stirring, for 2–3 minutes, or until they start to soften.

5 Add the chicken thighs to the frying pan and cook for 3–4 minutes, turning, until browned all over. Reduce the heat and add half the reserved marinade. Cover and cook for 15–20 minutes, adding more marinade when necessary.

6 Once the chicken is tender, add the balsamic vinegar and thyme and cook for a further 4 minutes.

7 Transfer the chicken and juices to 4 warmed serving plates and serve immediately with cooked polenta or rice.

NUTRITION
Calories *148*; Sugars *0.2 g*; Protein *11 g*;
Carbohydrate *0.2 g*; Fat *8 g*; Saturates *3 g*

 easy

 2 hrs 10 mins

35 mins

🍴 **COOK'S TIP**

To make the chicken thighs look neater, use wooden skewers to hold them together or secure them with a length of string.

Olives are a very popular flavouring for poultry and game in the Apulia region of Italy, where this recipe originally comes from.

Chicken *with* Green Olives

1 Heat the olive oil and the butter in a large frying pan over a medium heat. Add the chicken breasts and fry until golden brown all over. Remove the chicken from the pan.

2 Add the onion and garlic to the pan and fry until starting to soften. Add the peppers and mushrooms and cook for 2–3 minutes. Add the tomatoes and season to taste with salt and pepper. Transfer the vegetables to a casserole and arrange the chicken on top.

3 Add the wine to the frying pan and bring to the boil over a medium heat. Pour the wine over the chicken. Cover and cook the casserole in a preheated oven at 180°C/350°F/Gas Mark 4, for 50 minutes.

4 Add the olives to the casserole and mix in. Pour in the cream, cover and return to the oven for a further 10–20 minutes.

5 Meanwhile, bring a large saucepan of lightly salted water to the boil over a medium heat. Add the pasta and cook until tender, but still firm to the bite. Drain the pasta thoroughly, then transfer to a warmed serving dish.

6 Serve the chicken straight from the casserole dish with chopped parsley and the pasta served separately. Alternatively, arrange the chicken on top of the pasta, spoon over the sauce, garnish with parsley and serve.

SERVES 4

2 tbsp olive oil
25 g/1 oz butter
4 part boned chicken breasts
1 large onion, chopped finely
2 garlic cloves, crushed
2 red, yellow or green peppers, deseeded and cut into large pieces
250 g/9 oz button mushrooms, sliced or quartered
175 g/6 oz tomatoes, peeled and halved
150 ml/5 fl oz dry white wine
175 g/6 oz stoned green olives
4–6 tbsp double cream
400 g/14 oz dried pasta
salt and pepper
chopped fresh flat-leaf parsley, to garnish

NUTRITION
Calories 614; Sugars 6 g; Protein 34 g; Carbohydrate 49 g; Fat 30 g; Saturates 11 g

⭐⭐ easy
🕐 15 mins
🕐 1 hr 30 mins

This Italian-style dish is richly flavoured with pesto, which is a mixture of basil, olive oil, pine kernels and Parmesan cheese.

Grilled Chicken *with* Pesto Toasts

SERVES 4

2 quantities of Pesto Sauce (see page 128)
8 part-boned chicken thighs
1 tbsp olive oil for brushing
400 ml/14 fl oz passata
12 slices French bread
85 g/3 oz freshly grated Parmesan cheese
55 g/2 oz pine kernels or flaked almonds
assorted salad leaves, to serve

1 Make the Pesto Sauce (see page 128).

2 Arrange the chicken thighs in a single layer in a wide flameproof dish and brush lightly with olive oil. Cook under a preheated hot grill for 15 minutes, turning occasionally, until golden brown.

3 Insert a skewer into the thickest part of the meat to make sure there is no trace of pink in the juices.

4 Pour off any excess fat. Warm the passata and half the pesto sauce in a small saucepan and pour over the chicken. Cook for a few more minutes under the preheated hot grill, turning until the chicken is coated.

5 Meanwhile, spread the remaining pesto sauce on to the slices of bread. Arrange the bread over the chicken and sprinkle with the Parmesan cheese. Scatter the pine kernels over the cheese. Cook under the preheated hot grill for 2–3 minutes, or until browned and bubbling. Serve with salad leaves.

NUTRITION
Calories *787*; Sugars *6 g*; Protein *45 g*;
Carbohydrate *70 g*; Fat *38 g*; Saturates *9 g*

 easy

10 mins

25 mins

COOK'S TIP

Leaving the skin on means the chicken will have a higher fat content, but many people like the rich taste and crispy skin especially when it is blackened by the grill. The skin also keeps in the cooking juices.

This is a popular Italian classic in which browned chicken quarters are cooked in a tomato and pepper sauce.

Chicken Cacciatora

1 Rinse the chicken pieces under cold running water and pat dry with kitchen paper. Mix the flour and salt and pepper to taste on a plate, then lightly dust the chicken pieces with seasoned flour.

2 Heat the olive oil in a large frying pan over a medium heat. Add the chicken and fry until browned all over. Remove from the pan and reserve.

3 Drain off all but 2 tablespoons of the fat in the pan. Add the wine and stir for a few minutes, then add the peppers, carrots, celery and garlic. Season to taste with salt and pepper and simmer for about 15 minutes.

4 Add the chopped tomatoes to the pan. Cover and simmer for 30 minutes, stirring frequently, until the chicken is completely cooked through.

5 Transfer the chicken and sauce to 4 large, warmed serving plates and serve.

SERVES 4

1 roasting chicken, about 1.5 kg/3 lb 5 oz, cut into 6–8 serving pieces
125 g/4½ oz plain flour
3 tbsp olive oil
150 ml/5 fl oz dry white wine
1 green pepper, deseeded and sliced
1 red pepper, deseeded and sliced
1 carrot, chopped finely
1 celery stick, chopped finely
1 garlic clove, crushed
200 g/7 oz canned chopped tomatoes
salt and pepper

NUTRITION
Calories 397; Sugars 4 g; Protein 37 g; Carbohydrate 22 g; Fat 17 g; Saturates 4 g

    easy

    20 mins

1 hr

Chicken pieces are cooked in a succulent, mild mustard and lemon sauce, then coated in poppy seeds and served on a bed of fresh pasta shells.

Lemon Chicken Conchiglie

SERVES 4

8 chicken pieces, about 115 g/4 oz each
55 g/2 oz butter, melted
4 tbsp mild mustard (see Cook's Tip)
2 tbsp lemon juice
1 tbsp brown sugar
1 tsp paprika
3 tbsp poppy seeds
400 g/14 oz fresh pasta shells
1 tsp olive oil
salt and pepper

1 Arrange the chicken pieces, smooth-side down, in a single layer in a large ovenproof dish.

2 Mix the butter, mustard, lemon juice, sugar and paprika together in a bowl and season to taste with salt and pepper. Brush half the mixture over the upper surfaces of the chicken pieces and bake in a preheated oven at 200°C/400°F/ Gas Mark 6, for 15 minutes.

3 Remove the dish from the oven and carefully turn the chicken pieces over with tongs. Coat the upper surfaces of the chicken with the remaining mustard mixture, sprinkle the chicken pieces with poppy seeds and return to the oven for a further 15 minutes.

4 Meanwhile, bring a large saucepan of lightly salted water to the boil over a medium heat. Add the pasta shells and olive oil and cook for 8–10 minutes, or until tender, but still firm to the bite.

5 Drain the pasta thoroughly and arrange in a warmed serving dish. Top with the chicken, then pour over the sauce and serve immediately.

NUTRITION
Calories *652*; Sugars *5 g*; Protein *51 g*;
Carbohydrate *46 g*; Fat *31 g*; Saturates *12 g*

⭐⭐   easy
🕐   10 mins
🕐   35 mins

 COOK'S TIP

Dijon is the type of mustard most often used in cooking, as it has a clean and only mildly spicy flavour. German mustard has a sweet-sour taste, with Bavarian mustard being slightly sweeter. American mustard is mild and sweet.

Napoleon's chef was ordered to cook a sumptuous meal on the eve of the battle of Marengo – this feast of flavours was the result.

Chicken Marengo

1 Using a sharp knife, remove the bone from each of the chicken pieces.

2 Heat 1 tablespoon of olive oil in a large frying pan over a medium heat. Add the chicken pieces and cook for about 4–5 minutes, turning occasionally, or until browned all over.

3 Add the passata, wine and mixed herbs to the frying pan. Bring to the boil over a medium heat, then simmer for 30 minutes, or until the chicken is tender and the juices run clear when a skewer is inserted into the thickest part of the meat. Keep warm.

4 Mix the melted butter and garlic together. Lightly toast the slices of bread under a preheated hot grill and brush with the garlic butter. Keep warm.

5 Heat the remaining olive oil in a separate frying pan over a low heat. Add the mushrooms and cook for 2–3 minutes, or until just browned.

6 Add the olives and sugar to the chicken and cook until warmed through.

7 Transfer the chicken and sauce to 4 warmed serving plates. Garnish with fresh basil leaves and serve with the toast and fried mushrooms.

SERVES 4

8 chicken pieces
2 tbsp olive oil
300 g/10 fl oz passata
200 ml/7 fl oz white wine
2 tsp dried mixed herbs
40 g/1½ oz butter, melted
2 garlic cloves, crushed
8 slices white crusty bread
100 g/3½ oz mixed mushrooms (such as button, oyster and ceps)
40 g/1½ oz stoned black olives, chopped
1 tsp sugar
fresh basil leaves, to garnish

NUTRITION
Calories *521*; Sugars *6 g*; Protein *47 g*;
Carbohydrate *34 g*; Fat *19 g*; Saturates *8 g*

 moderate

20 mins

50 mins

A raspberry and honey sauce superbly counterbalances the richness of the duckling.

Duck *with* Raspberry Sauce

SERVES 4

4 boneless duckling breasts, about 275 g/
9½ oz each
25 g/1 oz butter
55 g/2 oz finely chopped carrots
55 g/2 oz finely chopped shallots
1 tbsp lemon juice
150 ml/5 fl oz chicken stock
4 tbsp clear honey
115 g/4 oz fresh or thawed frozen raspberries
25 g/1 oz plain flour
1 tbsp Worcestershire sauce
400 g/14 oz fresh linguine
salt and pepper

to garnish
fresh raspberries
fresh flat-leaf parsley sprigs

1 Trim and score the duck breasts with a sharp knife and season to taste with salt and pepper. Melt the butter in a frying pan over a medium heat. Add the duck breasts and fry until lightly coloured all over.

2 Add the carrots, shallots, lemon juice and half the chicken stock and simmer over a low heat for 1 minute. Stir in half the honey and half the raspberries. Sprinkle over half the flour and cook, stirring constantly, for 3 minutes. Season with pepper to taste, and add the Worcestershire sauce.

3 Stir in the remaining stock and cook for 1 minute. Stir in the remaining honey and remaining raspberries and sprinkle over the remaining flour. Cook for a further 3 minutes.

4 Remove the duck breasts from the pan and keep warm. Leave the sauce to simmer over a very low heat.

5 Meanwhile, bring a large saucepan of lightly salted water to the boil over a medium heat. Add the pasta and cook for 8–10 minutes, or until tender, but still firm to the bite. Drain and transfer to 4 warmed serving plates.

6 Slice the duck breast lengthways into 5-mm/¼-inch thick pieces. Pour a little sauce over the pasta and arrange the sliced duck in a fan shape on top of it. Garnish with a few fresh raspberries and flat-leaf parsley sprigs and serve.

NUTRITION
Calories *686*; Sugars *15 g*; Protein *62 g*;
Carbohydrate *70 g*; Fat *20 g*; Saturates *7 g*

easy

15 mins

25 mins

Partridge has a more delicate flavour than many game birds and this subtle sauce perfectly complements it.

Lime Partridge *with* Pesto

1 Make the Pesto Sauce (see page 128) and reserve until required.

2 Arrange the partridge pieces, smooth-side down, in a single layer in a large, ovenproof dish.

3 Mix the butter, Dijon mustard, lime juice and brown sugar together in a bowl. Season to taste with salt and pepper. Brush half of this mixture over the uppermost surfaces of the partridge pieces and bake in a preheated oven at 200°C/400°F/Gas Mark 6, for 15 minutes.

4 Remove the dish from the oven and coat the partridge pieces with half of the pesto sauce. Return to the oven and bake for a further 12 minutes.

5 Remove the dish from the oven and carefully turn the partridge pieces over and coat with the remaining mustard mixture. Return to the oven and bake for a further 10 minutes.

6 Meanwhile, bring a large saucepan of lightly salted water to the boil over a medium heat. Add the pasta and cook for about 10 minutes, or until tender, but still firm to the bite. Drain and transfer to a large serving dish. Toss the pasta with the remaining pesto sauce and the Parmesan cheese.

7 Serve the partridge with the pasta and pour over the cooking juices.

SERVES 4

1 quantity Pesto Sauce (see page 128)
8 partridge pieces, about 115 g/4 oz each
55 g/2 oz butter, melted
4 tbsp Dijon mustard
2 tbsp lime juice
1 tbsp brown sugar
450 g/1 lb dried rigatoni
115 g/4 oz freshly grated Parmesan cheese
salt and pepper

NUTRITION
Calories *895*; Sugars *5 g*; Protein *79 g*;
Carbohydrate *45 g*; Fat *45 g*; Saturates *18 g*

 challenging

15 mins

40 mins

Pasta *and* Rice

Pasta and rice are quick and easy to cook and, when combined with a variety of ingredients, can produce an enormous variety of dishes. To cook pasta, bring a saucepan of lightly salted water to the boil over a medium heat. Add the pasta and 1 teaspoon of olive oil, if you wish. Do not cover, but bring the water to a rolling boil. When the pasta is tender, but firm to the bite, drain and toss with butter, olive oil or sauce. As a rough guide, fresh unfilled pasta will take 3 minutes and filled fresh pasta 10 minutes to cook, while dried pasta will take approximately 10–15 minutes.

To cook a good quality rice like basmati, soak it for about 20–30 minutes to prevent the grains from sticking to each other. Add it to gently boiling, lightly salted water, stir once and cook until tender, but still firm to the bite. This will take 20 minutes. Allow 75 g/2¾ oz per person.

The original recipe takes about 4 hours to cook and should be left overnight to allow the flavours to mingle. This version is much quicker.

Spaghetti Bolognese

SERVES 4

1 tbsp olive oil
1 onion, chopped finely
2 garlic cloves, chopped
1 carrot, chopped
1 celery stick, chopped
50 g/1¾ oz pancetta or streaky bacon, diced
350 g/12 oz lean beef mince
400 g/14 oz canned chopped tomatoes
2 tsp dried oregano
125 ml/4 fl oz red wine
2 tbsp tomato purée
salt and pepper
650 g/1 lb 7 oz fresh spaghetti or 350 g/12 oz dried spaghetti
freshly grated Parmesan cheese, to serve (optional)

NUTRITION

Calories 591; Sugars 7 g; Protein 29 g;
Carbohydrate 640 g; Fat 24 g; Saturates 9 g

easy

20 mins

1 hr 5 mins

1 Heat the olive oil in a large frying pan over a medium heat. Add the onions and cook for 3 minutes.

2 Add the garlic, carrot, celery and pancetta or bacon and sauté over a fairly high heat for 3–4 minutes, or until just starting to brown.

3 Add the beef and cook over a high heat for a further 3 minutes, or until the meat is browned.

4 Stir in the tomatoes, oregano and red wine and bring to the boil over a medium heat. Reduce the heat and simmer for about 45 minutes.

5 Stir in the tomato purée and season to taste with salt and pepper.

6 Bring a large saucepan of lightly salted water to the boil over a medium heat. Add the pasta and cook for 8–10 minutes, or until tender, but still firm to the bite. Drain thoroughly.

7 Transfer the pasta to a serving plate and pour over the bolognese sauce. Toss to mix well and serve immediately with Parmesan cheese, if you wish.

COOK'S TIP

Try adding 25 g/1 oz dried porcini, soaked for 20 minutes in 2 tablespoons of warm water, to the bolognese sauce in step 4, if you wish.

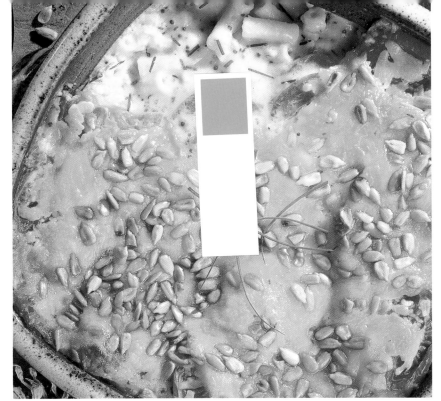

Based on a traditional family favourite, this pasta bake has plenty of flavour. Serve with a crisp salad for a simple, tasty supper.

Three-Cheese Macaroni

1 Make the Béchamel sauce (see page 14), transfer it to a bowl and cover with clingfilm to prevent a skin forming on the surface of the sauce. Reserve.

2 Bring a large saucepan of lightly salted water to the boil over a medium heat. Add the macaroni and cook for 8–10 minutes, or until just tender. Drain well and place in a lightly greased ovenproof dish.

3 Stir the beaten egg, Cheddar cheese, mustard and chives into the Béchamel sauce and season to taste with salt and pepper.

4 Spoon the sauce over the macaroni, making sure it is well covered. Arrange the sliced tomatoes in a layer over the top.

5 Sprinkle the red Leicester and blue cheeses and the sunflower seeds evenly over the pasta bake. Place the dish on a baking tray and bake in a preheated oven at 190°C/375°F/Gas Mark 5, for 25–30 minutes, or until the topping is bubbling and golden.

6 Garnish the pasta bake with snipped chives and serve immediately on 4 warmed plates.

SERVES 4

600 ml/1 pint Béchamel Sauce (see page 14)
225 g/8 oz dried macaroni
1 egg, beaten
125 g/4½ oz freshly grated mature
    Cheddar cheese
1 tbsp wholegrain mustard
2 tbsp snipped fresh chives
4 tomatoes, sliced
125 g/4½ oz freshly grated red
    Leicester cheese
55 g/2 oz freshly grated blue cheese
2 tbsp sunflower seeds
salt and pepper
snipped fresh chives, to garnish

NUTRITION
Calories *672*; Sugars *10 g*; Protein *31 g*;
Carbohydrate *40 g*; Fat *44 g*; Saturates *23 g*

✪✪✪   moderate
        30 mins
🕐   45 mins

These vegetable pancakes are tasty and filling, and look attractive served with a few oyster mushrooms and fried leek rings.

Macaroni *and* Corn Pancakes

SERVES 4

2 corn-on-the cobs
4 tbsp butter
115 g/4 oz red peppers, deseeded and finely diced
280 g/10 oz dried short-cut macaroni
150 ml/5 fl oz double cream
25 g/1 oz plain flour
4 egg yolks
4 tbsp olive oil
salt and pepper

to serve
oyster mushrooms
fried leeks

NUTRITION
Calories *702*; Sugars *4 g*; Protein *13 g*;
Carbohydrate *55 g*; Fat *50 g*; Saturates *23 g*

⭐⭐⭐   moderate
🕐   15 mins
🕐   40 mins

1 Bring a large saucepan of water to the boil over a medium heat. Add the corn-on-the cobs and cook for about 8 minutes. Drain thoroughly and refresh under cold running water for 3 minutes. Cut away the kernels on to kitchen paper and leave to dry.

2 Melt 2 tablespoons of the butter in a frying pan over a low heat. Add the peppers and cook for 4 minutes. Drain and pat dry on kitchen paper.

3 Bring a large saucepan of lightly salted water to the boil over a medium heat. Add the macaroni and cook for about 12 minutes, or until tender, but still firm to the bite. Drain the macaroni thoroughly and leave to cool in cold water until required.

4 Beat the cream with the flour, a pinch of salt and the egg yolks in a bowl until smooth. Add the corn and peppers. Drain the macaroni, then toss into the corn mixture. Season with pepper to taste.

5 Heat the remaining butter with the olive oil in a large frying pan over a medium heat. Drop spoonfuls of the mixture into the pan and press down to form flat pancakes. Fry until golden on both sides and the mixture is used. Drain on kitchen paper and serve with oyster mushrooms and fried leeks.

Fresh tomatoes make a delicious Italian-style sauce, which goes particularly well with all types of pasta.

Italian Tomato Sauce *and* Pasta

1 Heat the olive oil in a saucepan over a low heat. Add the onion and garlic and fry gently until soft.

2 Add the tomatoes, tomato purée and water. Season to taste with salt and pepper and bring to the boil over a low heat. Cover and simmer gently for about 10 minutes.

3 Meanwhile, bring a large saucepan of lightly salted water to the boil over a medium heat. Add the pasta and cook for 8–10 minutes, or until just tender, but still firm to the bite. Drain the pasta thoroughly and transfer to 4 warmed serving dishes.

4 Heat the bacon gently in a frying pan over a low heat until the fat runs, then add the mushrooms and cook for 3–4 minutes. Drain off any excess oil.

5 Add the bacon and mushrooms to the tomato mixture, together with the chopped parsley and the soured cream (if using). Reheat and serve immediately with the pasta.

SERVES 4

1 tbsp olive oil
1 small onion, chopped finely
1–2 garlic cloves, crushed
350 g/12 oz tomatoes, peeled and chopped
2 tsp tomato purée
2 tbsp water
300–350 g/10½–12 oz dried pasta shapes
85 g/3 oz lean bacon, derinded and diced
40 g/1½ oz mushrooms, sliced
1 tbsp chopped fresh parsley or 1 tsp chopped fresh coriander
2 tbsp soured cream or natural fromage frais, optional
salt and pepper

NUTRITION
Calories *304*; Sugars *8 g*; Protein *15 g*;
Carbohydrate *31 g*; Fat *14 g*; Saturates *5 g*

   very easy

   10 mins

   25 mins

The different shapes and textures of the vegetables make a mouthwatering presentation in this light and summery dish.

Broccoli *and* Asparagus Gemelli

SERVES 4

225 g/8 oz dried gemelli or other dried pasta shapes
1 head broccoli, cut into florets
2 courgettes, sliced
225 g/8 oz asparagus spears
115 g/4 oz mangetout
115 g/4 oz frozen peas
25 g/1 oz butter
3 tbsp vegetable stock
4 tbsp double cream
freshly grated nutmeg
2 tbsp chopped fresh parsley
2 tbsp fresh Parmesan cheese shavings
salt and pepper

1 Bring a large saucepan of lightly salted water to the boil over a medium heat. Add the pasta and cook for 8–10 minutes, or until tender, but still firm to the bite. Drain thoroughly, return to the saucepan, cover and keep warm.

2 Steam the broccoli, courgettes, asparagus spears and mangetout over a saucepan of boiling salted water until they are just starting to soften. Remove from the heat and refresh in cold water. Drain and reserve.

3 Bring a small saucepan of lightly salted water to the boil over a medium heat. Add the frozen peas and cook for 3 minutes. Drain the peas, refresh in cold water, then drain again. Reserve with the other vegetables.

4 Heat the butter and vegetable stock in a saucepan over a medium heat. Add all of the vegetables, reserving a few of the asparagus spears, and toss carefully with a wooden spoon until they have heated through, taking care not to break them up.

5 Stir in the cream and heat through without bringing to the boil. Season to taste with salt, pepper and nutmeg.

6 Transfer the pasta to a warmed serving dish and stir in the chopped parsley. Spoon over the vegetable sauce and sprinkle over the Parmesan cheese. Arrange the reserved asparagus spears in a pattern on the top and serve.

NUTRITION
Calories 517; Sugars 5 g; Protein 17 g;
Carbohydrate 42 g; Fat 32 g; Saturates 18 g

easy
10 mins
25 mins

Broccoli coated in a garlic-flavoured cream sauce, served on fresh herb tagliatelle. Try sprinkling with toasted pine kernels to add an extra crunch.

Pasta *with* Garlic *and* Broccoli

1 Cut the broccoli into even-sized florets. Bring a saucepan of lightly salted water to the boil over a medium heat. Add the broccoli, bring back to the boil and cook for 3 minutes, then drain thoroughly.

2 Place the soft cheese in a saucepan and heat over a low heat, stirring constantly, until melted. Add the milk and stir until well blended.

3 Add the broccoli to the cheese mixture and stir until the broccoli is coated.

4 Meanwhile, bring a large saucepan of lightly salted water to the boil over a medium heat. Add the pasta and cook for 3–4 minutes, or until tender, but still firm to the bite.

5 Drain the pasta thoroughly and transfer to 4 warmed serving plates. Spoon the broccoli and cheese sauce on top. Sprinkle with grated Parmesan cheese, garnish with snipped chives and serve immediately.

SERVES 4

500 g/1 lb 2 oz broccoli
300 g/10½ oz garlic and herb cream cheese
4 tbsp milk
350 g/12 oz fresh herb tagliatelle
25 g/1 oz freshly grated Parmesan cheese
salt
snipped fresh chives, to garnish

NUTRITION
Calories *424*; Sugars *3.5 g*; Protein *15 g*; Carbohydrate *39 g*; Fat *7.7 g*; Saturates *18 g*

easy

10 mins

15 mins

🍳 **COOK'S TIP**

A herb flavoured pasta goes particularly well with the broccoli sauce, but failing this, a tagliatelle verde or 'paglia e fieno' (literally 'straw and hay' – thin green and yellow noodles) will fit the bill.

A satisfying winter dish, this pasta and bean casserole with a crunchy topping is a slow-cooked, one-pot meal.

Casseroled Beans *and* Penne

SERVES 4

225 g/8 oz dried haricot beans, soaked overnight and drained
225 g/8 oz dried penne
850 ml/1½ pints vegetable stock
5 tbsp olive oil
2 large onions, sliced
2 garlic cloves, chopped
2 bay leaves
1 tsp dried oregano
1 tsp dried thyme
5 tbsp red wine
2 tbsp tomato purée
2 celery sticks, sliced
1 fennel bulb, sliced
115 g/4 oz sliced mushrooms
225 g/8 oz tomatoes, sliced
1 tsp dark muscovado sugar
4 tbsp dry white breadcrumbs
salt and pepper
salad leaves, to serve

NUTRITION

Calories *323*; Sugars *5 g*; Protein *13 g*;
Carbohydrate *41 g*; Fat *12 g*; Saturates *2 g*

moderate

25 mins

3 hrs 30 mins

1 Place the haricot beans in a large saucepan and pour over enough cold water to cover. Bring to the boil over a high heat and boil vigorously for 20 minutes. Drain thoroughly, reserve and keep warm.

2 Bring a large saucepan of lightly salted water to the boil over a medium heat. Add the pasta and cook for about 3 minutes. Drain the pasta thoroughly, reserve and keep warm.

3 Place the beans in a large, flameproof casserole dish. Add the vegetable stock and stir in the olive oil, the onions, garlic, bay leaves, oregano, thyme, wine and tomato purée. Bring to the boil over a medium heat, then cover and cook in a preheated oven at 180°C/350°F/Gas Mark 4, for 2 hours.

4 Add the pasta, celery, fennel, mushrooms and tomatoes to the casserole and season to taste with salt and pepper. Stir in the muscovado sugar and sprinkle over the breadcrumbs. Cover the dish and cook in the oven for 1 further hour.

5 Remove the casserole from the oven and transfer to 4 warmed serving plates and serve with salad leaves.

A Mediterranean mixture of red peppers, garlic and courgettes cooked in olive oil and tossed with pasta.

Pasta *and* Vegetable Sauce

1 Heat the olive oil in a heavy-based saucepan or flameproof casserole dish over a medium heat. Add the onion and garlic and cook, stirring occasionally, until the onion has softened. Add the peppers and courgettes and fry for 5 minutes, stirring occasionally.

2 Add the tomatoes, sun-dried tomato paste and basil. Season to taste with salt and pepper, cover and cook for 5 minutes.

3 Meanwhile, bring a large saucepan of lightly salted water to the boil over a medium heat. Add the pasta and cook for 3 minutes, or until just tender, but still firm to the bite. Drain thoroughly and add to the vegetables. Toss gently to mix well.

4 Place the mixture into a large, shallow ovenproof dish and sprinkle over the grated cheese.

5 Cook under a preheated hot grill for 5 minutes, or until the cheese is golden. Transfer to 4 warmed serving plates and garnish with basil sprigs. Serve.

SERVES 4

3 tbsp olive oil
1 onion, sliced
2 garlic cloves, chopped
3 red peppers, deseeded and cut into strips
3 courgettes, sliced
400 g/14 oz canned chopped tomatoes
3 tbsp sun-dried tomato purée
2 tbsp chopped fresh basil
225 g/8 oz fresh pasta spirals
125 g/4½ oz freshly grated Gruyère cheese
salt and pepper
fresh basil sprigs, to garnish

NUTRITION
Calories 341; Sugars 8 g; Protein 13 g;
Carbohydrate 30 g; Fat 20 g; Saturates 8 g

 very easy

 15 mins

 20 mins

 COOK'S TIP

Be careful not to overcook fresh pasta – it should be 'al dente' (retaining some 'bite'). It takes only a few minutes to cook as it is still full of moisture.

Delicious stirred into pasta, soups and salad dressings, pesto is available in most supermarkets, but making your own gives a much fresher, fuller flavour.

Pasta *with* Classic Pesto Sauce

SERVES 4

about 40 fresh basil leaves, washed and dried
3 garlic cloves, crushed
25 g/1 oz pine kernels
50 g/1¾ oz finely grated Parmesan cheese
3 tbsp extra virgin olive oil
salt and pepper
650 g/1 lb 7 oz fresh pasta or 350 g/12 oz dried pasta

1 Rinse the basil leaves in cold water and pat them dry on kitchen paper.

2 Place the basil leaves, garlic, pine kernels and grated Parmesan cheese in a food processor and blend for 30 seconds, or until smooth. Alternatively, pound the ingredients by hand, using a pestle and mortar.

3 If you are using a food processor, keep the motor running and slowly add the olive oil. Alternatively, add the olive oil drop by drop while stirring briskly. Season to taste with salt and pepper.

4 Meanwhile, bring a large saucepan of lightly salted water to the boil over a medium heat. Add the pasta and cook until tender, but still firm to the bite. Drain the pasta thoroughly.

5 Transfer the pasta to 4 large, warmed serving plates and serve with the pesto. Toss to mix well and serve immediately.

NUTRITION

Calories 155; Sugars 2.5 g; Protein 5.2 g; Carbohydrate 0.5 g; Fat 14.6 g; Saturates 8 g

 very easy

 15 mins

10 mins

COOK'S TIP

You can store pesto in the refrigerator for about 4 weeks. Cover the surface of the pesto with olive oil before sealing the container or bottle, to prevent the basil from oxidising and turning black.

This easy and satisfying Roman dish originated as a cheap meal for the impoverished, but is now a favourite in Italian restaurants and trattorias.

Garlic Spaghetti

1 Reserve 1 teaspoon of the olive oil and heat the remainder in a medium saucepan over a low heat. Add the garlic and a pinch of salt, stirring constantly, until golden brown, then remove the saucepan from the heat. Do not allow the garlic to burn as it will taint the flavour of the oil. (If it does burn, you will have to start all over again!)

2 Meanwhile, bring a large saucepan of lightly salted water to the boil over a medium heat. Add the pasta and remaining olive oil and cook for about 2–3 minutes, or until tender, but still firm to the bite. Drain the pasta thoroughly and return to the saucepan.

3 Add the olive oil and garlic mixture to the pasta and toss to coat thoroughly. Season with pepper to taste, add the chopped parsley and toss well to coat.

4 Transfer the pasta to 4 warmed serving dishes and serve immediately.

SERVES 4

125 ml/4 fl oz olive oil
3 garlic cloves, crushed
450 g/1 lb fresh spaghetti
3 tbsp roughly chopped fresh parsley
salt and pepper

NUTRITION
Calories *477*; Sugars *1.8 g*; Protein *0.6 g*; Carbohydrate *37 g*; Fat *40 g*; Saturates *3 g*

  easy

10 mins

10 mins

🍲 COOK'S TIP

It is worth buying the best-quality olive oil. Extra virgin oil is produced from the first pressing and has the lowest acidity. It is more expensive than other types of olive oil, but has the finest flavour.

This is a simple, clean-tasting dish of green vegetables, tofu and pasta, lightly tossed in olive oil.

Vegetables *and* Tofu

SERVES 4

225 g/8 oz asparagus
115 g/4 oz mangetout
225 g/8 oz French beans
1 leek
225 g/8 oz shelled small broad beans
300 g/10½ oz dried fusilli
2 tbsp olive oil
2 tbsp butter or margarine
1 garlic clove, crushed
225 g/8 oz tofu, cut into 2.5-cm/1-inch cubes (drained weight)
55 g/2 oz stoned green olives in brine, drained
salt and pepper
freshly grated Parmesan cheese, to serve

NUTRITION

Calories *400*; Sugars *5 g*; Protein *19 g*; Carbohydrate *46 g*; Fat *17 g*; Saturates *5 g*

easy

25 mins

20 mins

1 Cut the asparagus into 5-cm/2-inch lengths. Thinly slice the mangetout diagonally and slice the French beans into 2.5-cm/1-inch pieces. Thinly slice the leek.

2 Bring a large saucepan of water to the boil over a medium heat. Add the asparagus, green beans and broad beans. Bring back to the boil and cook for 4 minutes. Drain well, rinse in cold water and drain again. Reserve.

3 Bring a large saucepan of lightly salted water to the boil over a medium heat. Add the pasta and cook for 8–10 minutes, or until tender, but still firm to the bite. Drain thoroughly. Toss in 1 tablespoon of the olive oil and season to taste with salt and pepper.

4 Meanwhile, heat the remaining olive oil and the butter in a preheated wok or large frying pan over a low heat. Add the leek, garlic and tofu and cook gently for 1–2 minutes, or until the vegetables have just softened.

5 Stir in the mangetout and cook for 1 further minute.

6 Add the blanched vegetables and olives to the wok or frying pan and heat through for 1 minute. Carefully stir in the pasta and adjust the seasoning, if necessary. Cook for 1 minute and pile into a warmed serving dish. Serve immediately with Parmesan cheese.

A deliciously fresh and slightly spicy tomato sauce, which is excellent for lunch or a light supper.

Chilli Tagliatelle

1 Melt the butter in a large saucepan over a medium heat. Add the onion and garlic and cook for 3–4 minutes, or until softened.

2 Add the chillies to the saucepan and continue cooking for about 2 minutes.

3 Add the tomatoes and stock, then reduce the heat to low and simmer for about 10 minutes, stirring constantly.

4 Pour the sauce into a food processor and process for 1 minute, or until smooth. Alternatively, rub the sauce through a sieve.

5 Return the sauce to the saucepan and add the tomato purée, sugar, and salt and pepper to taste. Gently reheat over a low heat, until piping hot.

6 Bring a large saucepan of lightly salted water to the boil over a medium heat. Add the pasta and cook until tender, but still firm to the bite. Drain the pasta thoroughly, transfer to 4 large, warmed serving plates and serve immediately with the sauce.

SERVES 4

50 g/1¾ oz butter
1 onion, chopped finely
1 garlic clove, crushed
2 small fresh red chillies, deseeded and diced
450 g/1 lb fresh tomatoes, peeled, deseeded and diced
200 ml/7 fl oz vegetable stock
2 tbsp tomato purée
1 tsp sugar
650 g/1 lb 7 oz fresh green and white tagliatelle, or 350 g/12 oz dried tagliatelle
salt and pepper

NUTRITION
Calories *306*; Sugars *7 g*; Protein *8 g*;
Carbohydrate *45 g*; Fat *12 g*; Saturates *7 g*

easy

15 mins

35 mins

COOK'S TIP

Try topping your pasta dish with 50 g/1¼ oz pancetta or unsmoked bacon, diced and dry-fried for about 5 minutes, or until crispy.

These delicious individual pasta puddings are served with a tasty tomato and bay leaf sauce.

Pasta *and* Cheese Puddings

SERVES   4

15 g/½ oz butter or margarine, softened
55 g/2 oz dried white breadcrumbs
175 g/6 oz dried tricolour spaghetti
300 ml/10 fl oz Béchamel Sauce
   (see page 14)
1 egg yolk
125 g/4½ oz freshly grated Gruyère cheese
salt and pepper
4 fresh flat-leaf parsley sprigs, to garnish

tomato sauce

2 tsp olive oil
1 onion, chopped finely
1 bay leaf
150 ml/5 fl oz dry white wine
150 ml/5 fl oz passata
1 tbsp tomato purée

NUTRITION
Calories 517; Sugars *8 g*; Protein *19 g*;
Carbohydrate *47 g*; Fat *27 g*; Saturates *13 g*

⭐⭐⭐   moderate

🕐   45 mins

🕐   50 mins

1 Grease four 175-ml/6 fl-oz moulds or ramekins with the butter or margarine. Evenly coat the insides with half the breadcrumbs.

2 Break the pasta into 5-cm/2-inch lengths. Bring a saucepan of lightly salted water to the boil over a medium heat. Add the pasta and cook for about 5–6 minutes, or until just tender, but still firm to the bite. Drain thoroughly and place in a bowl.

3 Mix the Béchamel Sauce (see page 14), egg yolk and cheese into the cooked pasta. Season to taste with salt and pepper and pack into the moulds.

4 Sprinkle the puddings with the remaining breadcrumbs and place the moulds on a large baking tray. Bake in a preheated oven at 220°C/425°F/Gas Mark 7, for 20 minutes, or until golden. Leave to stand for 10 minutes.

5 Meanwhile, make the sauce. Heat the olive oil in a large frying pan over a medium heat. Add the onion and bay leaf and fry for 2–3 minutes, or until the onion is just softened.

6 Stir in the wine, passata, tomato purée and season to taste. Bring the sauce to the boil and simmer for 20 minutes, or until thickened. Remove from the heat and discard the bay leaf.

7 Run a palette knife around the inside of the moulds. Turn the puddings out on to 4 serving plates, garnish with parsley sprigs and serve with the sauce.

This mouthwatering dish would make an excellent light lunch for four people, or a good starter for six.

Walnut *and* Olive Pasta

1 Place the bread in a shallow dish, pour over the milk, then leave to soak until the liquid is absorbed.

2 Spread the walnuts out on a baking tray and toast in a preheated oven at 190°C/375°F/Gas Mark 5, for about 5 minutes, or until golden. Leave to cool.

3 Place the soaked bread, walnuts, garlic, olives, Parmesan cheese and 6 tablespoons of the olive oil in a food processor and process until a purée forms. Season to taste with salt and pepper, then stir in the cream.

4 Bring a large saucepan of lightly salted water to the boil over a medium heat. Add the pasta and cook for 2–3 minutes, or until tender, but still firm to the bite. Drain the pasta thoroughly and toss with the remaining olive oil.

5 Transfer the pasta to warmed serving plates and spoon the olive, garlic and walnut sauce on top. Sprinkle over the chopped parsley and serve.

SERVES 4 – 6

2 thick slices wholemeal bread, crusts removed
300 ml/10 fl oz milk
275 g/9½ oz shelled walnuts
2 garlic cloves, crushed
115 g/4 oz stoned black olives
55 g/2 oz freshly grated Parmesan cheese
8 tbsp extra virgin olive oil
150 ml/5 fl oz double cream
450 g/1 lb fresh fettuccine
2–3 tbsp chopped fresh parsley
salt and pepper

NUTRITION
Calories *833*; Sugars *5 g*; Protein *20 g*; Carbohydrate *44 g*; Fat *66 g*; Saturates *15 g*

COOK'S TIP

Grated Parmesan cheese quickly loses its pungency. It is better to buy solid cheese and grate it when needed. Wrapped in tinfoil, Parmesan cheese will keep in the refrigerator for several months.

 easy

 15 mins

15 mins

10 mins

This light pasta dish has a delicate flavour ideally suited to a summer lunch.

Spaghetti *with* Ricotta Cheese

SERVES 4

350 g/12 oz dried spaghetti
3 tbsp butter
2 tbsp chopped fresh flat-leaf parsley
1 tbsp pine kernels
salt and pepper
1 fresh flat-leaf parsley sprig, to garnish

ricotta cheese sauce
125 g/4½ oz freshly ground almonds
125 g/4½ oz ricotta cheese
pinch of freshly grated nutmeg
pinch of ground cinnamon
150 ml/5 fl oz crème fraîche
2 tbsp olive oil
125 ml/4 fl oz hot chicken stock

1 Bring a large saucepan of lightly salted water to the boil over a medium heat. Add the pasta and cook for about 8–10 minutes, or until tender, but still firm to the bite.

2 Drain the pasta thoroughly, return to the saucepan and toss with the butter and chopped parsley. Reserve and keep warm.

3 To make the sauce, mix the ground almonds, ricotta cheese, nutmeg, cinnamon and crème fraîche together in a small saucepan over a low heat until it forms a thick paste. Gradually stir in the oil. When the oil has been fully incorporated, gradually stir in the hot chicken stock, until smooth. Season with pepper to taste.

4 Transfer the pasta to a warmed serving dish, pour over the sauce and toss together well with 2 forks (see Cook's Tip). Sprinkle over the pine kernels, garnish with a flat-leaf parsley sprig and serve immediately.

NUTRITION

Calories *701*; Sugars *12 g*; Protein *17 g*; Carbohydrate *73 g*; Fat *40 g*; Saturates *15 g*

⭐⭐   easy
🕐   5 mins
🕐   25 mins

 COOK'S TIP

Use 2 large forks to toss spaghetti or other long pasta, as this ensures that the pasta is thoroughly coated with the sauce. Special spaghetti forks are available from some cookware departments and large kitchen shops.

The tasty flavours and delightful textures of artichoke hearts and black olives make a winning combination.

Artichoke *and* Olive Spaghetti

1 Heat 1 tablespoon of the olive oil in a large frying pan over a low heat. Add the onion, garlic, lemon juice and aubergines and gently fry for 4–5 minutes, or until lightly browned.

2 Pour in the passata, season to taste with salt and pepper and add the sugar and tomato purée. Bring to the boil over a medium heat, then reduce the heat and simmer for 20 minutes.

3 Gently stir in the artichoke halves and olives and cook for 5 minutes.

4 Meanwhile, bring a large saucepan of lightly salted water to the boil over a medium heat. Add the pasta and cook for 8–10 minutes, or until just tender, but still firm to the bite. Drain thoroughly, toss in the remaining olive oil and season to taste with salt and pepper.

5 Transfer the pasta to 4 warmed serving bowls and top with the vegetable sauce. Garnish with basil sprigs and serve immediately.

SERVES 4

2 tbsp olive oil
1 large red onion, chopped
2 garlic cloves, crushed
1 tbsp lemon juice
4 baby aubergines, quartered
600 ml/1 pint passata
2 tsp caster sugar
2 tbsp tomato purée
400 g/14 oz canned artichoke hearts, drained and halved
125 g/4½ oz stoned black olives
350 g/12 oz wholewheat dried spaghetti
salt and pepper
fresh basil sprigs, to garnish

NUTRITION
Calories 393; Sugars 11 g; Protein 14 g; Carbohydrate 63 g; Fat 11 g; Saturates 2 g

⭐⭐ easy
🕐 20 mins
🕐 35 mins

This delicious roasted pepper and chilli sauce is sweet and spicy.

Fusilli Salad *with* Chilli

SERVES 4

2 red peppers, halved and deseeded
1 small fresh red chilli
2 garlic cloves
4 tomatoes, halved
50 g/1¾ oz ground almonds
7 tbsp olive oil
650 g/1 lb 7 oz fresh pasta or 350 g/12 oz dried pasta
fresh oregano leaves, to garnish

NUTRITION
Calories *423*; Sugars *5 g*; Protein *9 g*;
Carbohydrate *38 g*; Fat *27 g*; Saturates *4 g*

⭐⭐⭐   moderate

🕑   25 mins

🕐   30 mins

1 Place the peppers, skin-side up, on a baking tray with the chilli, garlic and tomatoes, skin-side down. Cook under a preheated hot grill for about 10–15 minutes, or until the skins are charred and blistered. After 8 minutes, turn the tomatoes skin-side up.

2 Place the peppers and chilli in a polythene bag and leave to sweat for about 10 minutes. Remove the skin from the peppers and deseed and skin the chilli. Using a sharp knife, slice the flesh into strips.

3 Peel the garlic and peel and deseed the tomatoes.

4 Place the almonds on a baking tray and cook under the preheated hot grill for 2–3 minutes, or until golden.

5 Place the pepper, chilli, garlic and tomatoes in a food processor and process until a purée forms. Keep the motor running and slowly add the olive oil to form a thick sauce. Alternatively, mash the mixture with a fork and beat in the olive oil, drop by drop.

6 Stir the toasted ground almonds into the mixture. Place the sauce in a saucepan and warm until it is heated through.

7 Bring a large saucepan of lightly salted water to the boil over a medium heat. Add the pasta and cook until tender, but still firm to the bite. Drain the pasta and transfer to 4 serving dishes. Pour over the sauce and toss to mix. Garnish with fresh oregano leaves and serve.

Simple and inexpensive, this tasty dish is fairly quick and easy to prepare, but looks very impressive.

Pasta *with* Nuts *and* Cheese

1 Scatter the pine kernels on to a baking tray and cook under a preheated hot grill, turning occasionally, until lightly browned all over. Reserve.

2 Bring a large saucepan of lightly salted water to the boil over a medium heat. Add the pasta and cook for 8–10 minutes, or until tender, but still firm to the bite.

3 Meanwhile, cook the courgettes and broccoli in a small amount of boiling, lightly salted water for about 5 minutes, or until just tender.

4 Place the soft cheese in a saucepan and heat gently over a low heat, stirring constantly. Add the milk and stir. Add the basil and mushrooms and cook gently for 2–3 minutes. Stir in the blue cheese and season to taste with salt and pepper.

5 Drain the pasta and vegetables and mix together in a serving dish. Pour the sauce over and add the pine kernels. Using 2 forks, toss the pasta gently to mix. Garnish with a basil sprig and serve immediately with salad leaves.

SERVES 4

55 g/2 oz pine kernels
350 g/12 oz dried pasta shapes
2 courgettes, sliced
125 g/4½ oz broccoli, broken into florets
200 g/7 oz full-fat soft cheese
150 ml/5 fl oz milk
1 tbsp chopped fresh basil
125 g/4½ oz button mushrooms, sliced
85 g/3 oz blue cheese, crumbled
salt and pepper
1 fresh basil sprig, to garnish
mixed salad leaves, to serve

NUTRITION

Calories 531; Sugars 4 g; Protein 20 g; Carbohydrate 35 g; Fat 35 g; Saturates 16 g

⭐⭐ easy

🕐 10 mins

🕐 30 mins

The pappardelle and vegetables are tossed in a delicious chilli and tomato sauce for a quick and economical meal.

Pasta *and* Chilli Tomatoes

SERVES 4

275 g/9½ oz pappardelle
3 tbsp groundnut oil
2 garlic cloves, crushed
2 shallots, sliced
225 g/8 oz green beans, sliced
100 g/3½ oz cherry tomatoes, halved
1 tsp crushed chillies
4 tbsp crunchy peanut butter
150 ml/5 fl oz coconut milk
1 tbsp tomato purée

1 Bring a large saucepan of lightly salted water to the boil over a medium heat. Add the pasta and cook for 5–6 minutes, or until tender, but still firm to the bite. Drain the pasta thoroughly, reserve and keep warm.

2 Heat the groundnut oil in a large frying pan or preheated wok over a medium heat. Add the garlic and shallots and stir-fry for 1 minute.

3 Add the green beans and drained pasta to the frying pan or wok and stir-fry for 5 minutes. Add the cherry tomatoes and mix well.

4 Mix the crushed chillies, peanut butter, coconut milk and tomato purée together. Pour the chilli mixture into the frying pan or wok, toss well and heat through.

5 Transfer the pasta to 4 warmed serving dishes and serve immediately.

NUTRITION

Calories *353*; Sugars *7 g*; Protein *10 g*;
Carbohydrate *26 g*; Fat *24 g*; Saturates *4 g*

⭐ very easy

🕐 15 mins

🕐 20 mins

👨‍🍳 **COOK'S TIP**

Add slices of chicken or beef to the recipe and stir-fry with the beans and pasta in step 5 for a more substantial main meal.

The smoked salmon ideally complements the spaghetti to give a very luxurious dish.

Spaghetti *and* Salmon Sauce

1 Bring a large saucepan of lightly salted water to the boil over a medium heat. Add the pasta and cook for 8–10 minutes, or until tender, but still firm to the bite. Drain the pasta thoroughly, return to the saucepan, sprinkle over the olive oil, cover and shake well. Reserve and keep warm until required.

2 To make the sauce, heat the cream and the whisky or brandy in separate small saucepans to simmering point. Do not let them boil.

3 Mix the cream with the whisky or brandy in a bowl.

4 Cut the smoked salmon into thin strips and add to the cream mixture. Season to taste with a little pepper and cayenne pepper, and then stir in the chopped coriander.

5 Transfer the pasta to a warmed serving dish, pour on the sauce and toss thoroughly, using 2 large forks. Scatter the crumbled feta cheese over the pasta and garnish with the chopped coriander or parsley. Serve immediately.

SERVES 4

500 g/1 lb 2 oz dried buckwheat spaghetti
2 tbsp olive oil
85 g/3 oz feta cheese, crumbled (drained weight)
1 tbsp chopped fresh coriander or parsley, to garnish

salmon sauce
300 ml/10 fl oz double cream
150 ml/5 fl oz whisky or brandy
125 g/4½ oz smoked salmon
large pinch of cayenne pepper
2 tbsp chopped fresh coriander or parsley
salt and pepper

NUTRITION
Calories *782*; Sugars *3 g*; Protein *20 g*; Carbohydrate *48 g*; Fat *48 g*; Saturates *27 g*

 very easy
 10 mins
10 mins
15 mins

Frozen peeled prawns from the freezer can become the star ingredient in this colourful dish.

Spaghetti *and* Shellfish

SERVES 4

225 g/8 oz short-cut spaghetti, or
   long spaghetti broken into 15-cm/
   6-inch lengths
2 tbsp olive oil
300 ml/10 fl oz chicken stock
1 tsp lemon juice
1 small cauliflower, cut into florets
2 carrots, sliced thinly
125 g/4½ oz mangetout, trimmed
55 g/2 oz butter
1 onion, sliced
225 g/8 oz courgettes, sliced thinly
1 garlic clove, chopped
350 g/12 oz frozen peeled prawns, thawed
2 tbsp chopped fresh parsley
25 g/1 oz freshly grated Parmesan cheese
½ tsp paprika
salt and pepper
4 whole prawns, to garnish (optional)

NUTRITION
Calories *510*; Sugars *38 g*; Protein *33 g*;
Carbohydrate *44 g*; Fat *24 g*; Saturates *11 g*

      moderate
          35 mins
          30 mins

1 Bring a large saucepan of lightly salted water to the boil over a medium heat. Add the pasta and cook for 8–10 minutes, or until tender, but still firm to the bite. Drain thoroughly, then return to the saucepan and stir in the olive oil. Cover and keep warm.

2 Bring the chicken stock and lemon juice to the boil over a medium heat. Add the cauliflower and carrots and cook for 3–4 minutes, or until barely tender. Remove with a slotted spoon and reserve. Add the mangetout and cook for 1–2 minutes, until they start to soften. Remove with a slotted spoon and add to the other vegetables. Reserve the stock for future use.

3 Melt half the butter in a frying pan over a medium heat. Add the onion and courgettes and fry for about 3 minutes. Add the garlic and prawns and cook for a further 2–3 minutes, or until thoroughly heated through.

4 Stir in the reserved vegetables and heat through. Season to taste with salt and pepper, then stir in the remaining butter.

5 Transfer the pasta to a serving dish. Pour on the sauce and sprinkle with parsley. Using 2 forks, toss, until coated. Sprinkle with Parmesan cheese and paprika and garnish with the prawns (if using). Serve immediately.

Fresh clams are available from most good fishmongers. If you prefer, use canned clams, which are less messy to eat but not so pretty to serve.

Pasta *with* Clams *and* White Wine

1 If you are using fresh clams, scrub them clean and discard any that are already open.

2 Heat the olive oil in a large frying pan over a medium heat. Add the garlic and clams to the pan and cook for 2 minutes, shaking the pan to ensure that all the clams are coated in the oil.

3 Add the remaining seafood mixture to the pan and cook for a further 2 minutes.

4 Pour the wine and stock over the seafood. Bring to the boil over a medium heat. Cover, reduce the heat and simmer for 8–10 minutes, or until the shells open. Discard any shells that are still closed.

5 Meanwhile, bring a large saucepan of lightly salted water to the boil over a medium heat. Add the pasta and cook until tender, but still firm to the bite. Drain thoroughly.

6 Stir the tarragon into the sauce and season to taste with salt and pepper.

7 Transfer the pasta to a serving plate and pour over the sauce. Serve.

 COOK'S TIP

Red clam sauce can be made by adding 8 tablespoons of passata to the sauce along with the stock in step 4. Follow the same cooking method.

SERVES 4

650 g/1 lb 7 oz oz fresh clams or
   280 g/10 oz canned clams, drained
2 tbsp olive oil
2 garlic cloves, chopped finely
400 g/14 oz mixed seafood, such as prawns,
   squid and mussels, thawed if frozen
150 ml/5 fl oz white wine
150 ml/5 fl oz fish stock
650 g/1 lb 7 oz fresh pasta or
   350 g/12 oz dried pasta
2 tbsp chopped tarragon
salt and pepper

NUTRITION
Calories *410*; Sugars *1 g*; Protein *39 g*;
Carbohydrate *39 g*; Fat *9 g*; Saturates *1 g*

⭐⭐   easy

🕐   20 mins

🕐   20 mins

The creamy, nutty flavour of squash complements the 'al dente' texture of the pasta perfectly. This recipe has been adapted for the microwave.

Penne *and* Butternut Squash

SERVES 4

2 tbsp olive oil
1 garlic clove, crushed
55 g/2 oz fresh white breadcrumbs
500 g/1 lb 2 oz butternut squash, peeled and deseeded
8 tbsp water
500 g/1 lb 2 oz fresh penne, or other pasta shapes
15 g/½ oz butter
1 onion, sliced
125 g/4½ oz ham, cut into strips
200 ml/7 fl oz single cream
55 g/2 oz freshly grated Cheddar cheese
2 tbsp chopped fresh parsley
salt and pepper

1 Mix the olive oil, garlic and breadcrumbs together and spread out on a large plate. Cook in the microwave on High power for 4–5 minutes, stirring every minute, until crisp and starting to brown. Reserve.

2 Dice the squash, then place in a large bowl with half the water. Cover and cook on High power for 8–9 minutes, stirring occasionally. Leave to stand for 2 minutes.

3 Place the pasta in a large bowl, add a little salt and pour over enough boiling water to cover by 2.5 cm/1 inch. Cover and cook on High power for 5 minutes, stirring once, until the pasta is just tender, but still firm to the bite. Leave to stand, covered, for 1 minute before draining.

4 Place the butter and onion in a large bowl. Cover and cook on High power for 3 minutes.

5 Using a fork, coarsely mash the squash. Add to the onion with the pasta, ham, cream, cheese, parsley and remaining water. Season generously and mix well. Cover and cook on High power for 4 minutes, until heated through.

6 Transfer the pasta to a large, warmed serving dish, sprinkle with the crisp garlic crumbs and serve.

NUTRITION
Calories *499*; Sugars *4 g*; Protein *20 g*;
Carbohydrate *49 g*; Fat *26 g*; Saturates *13 g*

easy

15 mins

30 mins

These large pasta nests look very impressive filled with grilled mixed vegetables, and taste absolutely delicious.

Vegetable Pasta Nests

1 Bring a large saucepan of lightly salted water to the boil over a medium heat. Add the pasta and cook for 8–10 minutes, or until just tender, but still firm to the bite. Drain thoroughly and reserve until required.

2 Place the aubergine, courgette and pepper on a baking tray.

3 Mix the oil and garlic together in a small bowl and pour over the vegetables, tossing to coat thoroughly.

4 Cook the vegetables under a preheated hot grill for 10 minutes, turning occasionally, until tender and lightly charred. Reserve and keep warm.

5 Transfer the pasta to 4 lightly greased Yorkshire pudding tins. Using 2 forks, curl the pasta to form nests.

6 Brush the pasta nests with a little melted butter and sprinkle with the breadcrumbs. Bake in a preheated oven at 200°C/400°F/Gas Mark 6, for 15 minutes, or until lightly golden. Remove the pasta nests from the tins and transfer to 4 serving plates. Divide the grilled vegetables between the nests, season to taste with salt and pepper and garnish with parsley sprigs. Serve.

SERVES 4

175 g/6 oz dried spaghetti
1 aubergine, halved and sliced
1 courgette, diced
1 red pepper, deseeded and
    diagonally chopped
6 tbsp olive oil
2 garlic cloves, crushed
4 tbsp butter or margarine, melted,
    plus extra for greasing
15 g/¹⁄₂ oz dry white breadcrumbs
salt and pepper
4 fresh parsley sprigs, to garnish

NUTRITION
Calories *392*; Sugars *1 g*; Protein *6 g*;
Carbohydrate *32 g*; Fat *28 g*; Saturates *6 g*

  moderate

25 mins

40 mins

🍳 **COOK'S TIP**

The Italian term *al dente* means 'to the bite' and describes cooked pasta that is not too soft, but still has a 'bite' to it.

A recipe that has both Italian and Greek origins, this dish may be served hot or cold, cut into thick, satisfying squares.

Pasticcio

SERVES 6

225 g/8 oz dried fusilli, or other pasta shapes
4 tbsp double cream
salt and pepper
fresh rosemary sprigs, to garnish

sauce

2 tbsp olive oil, plus extra for brushing
1 onion, sliced thinly
1 red pepper, deseeded and chopped
2 garlic cloves, chopped
600 g/1 lb 5 oz lean beef mince
400 g/14 oz canned chopped tomatoes
125 ml/4 fl oz dry white wine
2 tbsp chopped fresh parsley
50 g/1¾ oz canned anchovy fillets, drained
   and chopped

topping

300 ml/10 fl oz natural yogurt
3 eggs
pinch of freshly grated nutmeg
40 g/1½ oz freshly grated Parmesan cheese

NUTRITION
Calories *590*; Sugars *8 g*; Protein *34 g*;
Carbohydrate *23 g*; Fat *39 g*; Saturates *16 g*

easy

35 mins

1 hr 15 mins

1 To make the sauce, heat the olive oil in a large frying pan over a medium heat. Add the onion and red pepper and fry for 3 minutes. Stir in the garlic and cook for 1 further minute. Stir in the beef and cook, stirring frequently, until browned.

2 Add the tomatoes and wine, stir well and bring to the boil over a medium heat. Simmer for 20 minutes, or until the sauce is fairly thick. Stir in the parsley and anchovies and season to taste with salt and pepper.

3 Bring a large saucepan of lightly salted water to the boil over a medium heat. Add the pasta and cook for 8–10 minutes, or until tender, but still firm to the bite. Drain thoroughly, then transfer to a large bowl. Stir in the cream and reserve.

4 To make the topping, beat the yogurt and eggs together and season to taste with nutmeg, salt and pepper.

5 Brush a large, shallow baking dish with olive oil. Spoon in half the pasta mixture and cover with half the meat sauce. Repeat these layers, then spread the topping evenly over the final layer. Sprinkle the Parmesan cheese evenly on top.

6 Bake in a preheated oven at 190°C/ 375°F/Gas Mark 5, for 25 minutes, or until the topping is golden brown and bubbling. Garnish with a few rosemary sprigs and serve.

These tasty little squares of pasta stuffed with mushrooms and cheese are surprisingly filling. Serve about 3 pieces for a starter and up to 9 for a main course.

Cheesy Pasta Squares

1 Using a serrated pasta cutter, cut 5-cm/2-inch squares from the sheets of fresh pasta. To make 36 pasta squares, you will need 72 squares. Once the pasta is cut, cover the squares with clingfilm to stop them drying out.

2 Heat 25 g/1 oz of the butter in a frying pan over a low heat. Add the shallots, 1 crushed garlic clove, mushrooms and celery and cook for 4–5 minutes.

3 Remove the pan from the heat, stir in the cheese and season to taste with salt and pepper.

4 Spoon ½ teaspoon of the mixture on to the centre of 36 pasta squares. Brush the edges of the squares with water and top with the remaining 36 squares. Press the edges together to seal. Leave to rest for 5 minutes.

5 Bring a large saucepan of water to the boil over a medium heat. Add the olive oil and cook the pasta squares, in batches, for 2–3 minutes. The pasta squares will rise to the surface when cooked and the pasta should be tender with a slight bite. Remove from the pan with a slotted spoon and drain thoroughly.

6 Meanwhile, melt the remaining butter in a saucepan over a low heat. Add the remaining garlic and plenty of pepper and cook for 1–2 minutes.

7 Transfer the pasta squares to 4 serving plates and pour over the garlic butter. Garnish with the pecorino cheese and serve immediately.

S E R V E S   4

about 300 g/10½ oz thin sheets of fresh pasta
75 g/2¾ oz butter
50 g/1¾ oz shallots, chopped finely
3 garlic cloves, crushed
50 g/1¾ oz mushrooms, wiped and finely chopped
½ celery stick, chopped finely
25 g/1 oz pecorino cheese, finely grated, plus extra to garnish
1 tbsp oil
salt and pepper

N U T R I T I O N
Calories *360*; Sugars *1 g*; Protein *9 g*; Carbohydrate *36 g*; Fat *21 g*; Saturates *12 g*

 challenging

 1 hr 15 mins

25 mins

Spinach ribbon noodles covered with a rich tomato sauce and topped with creamy chicken make a very appetising dish.

Tagliatelle *and* Chicken Sauce

SERVES 4

Basic Tomato Sauce (see page 14)
650 g/1 lb 7 oz fresh green tagliatelle or 350 g/12 oz dried green tagliatelle
salt
fresh basil leaves, to garnish

chicken sauce

55 g/2 oz unsalted butter
400 g/14 oz skinless boneless chicken breasts, sliced thinly
85 g/3 oz blanched almonds
300 ml/10 fl oz double cream
salt and pepper

1 Make the tomato sauce (see page 14), reserve and keep warm.

2 To make the chicken sauce, melt the butter in a large, heavy-based frying pan over a medium heat. Add the chicken strips and almonds and cook, stirring frequently, for 5–6 minutes, or until the chicken is cooked through.

3 Meanwhile, pour the cream into a small saucepan, set over a low heat and bring to the boil. Boil for 10 minutes until reduced by almost half. Pour the cream over the chicken and almonds, stir well and season to taste with salt and pepper. Remove the saucepan from the heat, reserve and keep warm.

4 Bring a large saucepan of lightly salted water to the boil over a medium heat. Add the pasta and cook until tender, but still firm to the bite. Fresh tagliatelle will take 2–3 minutes and dried pasta will take 8–10 minutes. Drain thoroughly, then return to the pan, cover and keep warm.

5 When ready to serve, transfer the pasta to a warmed serving dish and spoon the tomato sauce over it. Spoon the chicken and cream into the centre, sprinkle with the basil leaves and serve immediately.

NUTRITION

Calories *853*; Sugars *6 g*; Protein *32 g*;
Carbohydrate *23 g*; Fat *71 g*; Saturates *34 g*

easy

30 mins

25 mins

147

PASTA & RICE

If preferred, ordinary long-grain rice can be used instead of arborio rice, but it won't give you the traditional, deliciously creamy texture that is typical of Italian risottos.

Italian Risotto

1 Heat the sunflower oil and butter in a large, heavy-based saucepan over a medium-low heat. Add the leek and yellow pepper and cook for 1 minute. Add the chicken and cook, stirring constantly, until golden brown.

2 Stir in the rice and cook for 2–3 minutes. Add the saffron strands and season to taste with salt and pepper.

3 Add the stock, a little at a time, and cook over a low heat, stirring constantly, for about 20 minutes, or until the rice is tender and most of the liquid has been absorbed. Do not let the risotto dry out – add more stock, if necessary.

4 Stir in the sweetcorn, peanuts and grated Parmesan cheese, then adjust the seasoning to taste, if necessary. Transfer to 4 warmed serving plates and serve immediately.

SERVES 4

2 tbsp sunflower oil
15 g/½ oz butter or margarine
1 leek, sliced thinly
1 large yellow pepper, deseeded and diced
3 skinless, boneless chicken breasts, diced
350 g/12 oz arborio rice, rinsed
few strands of saffron
1.5 litres/2¾ pints hot chicken stock
200 g/7 oz canned sweetcorn
55 g/2 oz toasted unsalted peanuts
55 g/2 oz freshly grated Parmesan cheese
salt and pepper

NUTRITION
Calories 701; Sugars 7 g; Protein 35 g;
Carbohydrate 88 g; Fat 26 g; Saturates 8 g

  easy

10 mins

30 mins

COOK'S TIP

Risottos can be frozen for up to 1 month before adding the Parmesan cheese, but remember to reheat this risotto thoroughly as it contains chicken.

The Genoese risotto is cooked in a different way from any of the other risottos. First, you cook the rice, then you prepare a sauce, then you mix the two together. The final result, however, is just as delicious!

Mixed Seafood Risotto

SERVES 4

1.2 litres/2 pints hot fish or chicken stock
350 g/12 oz arborio rice, rinsed
50 g/1¾ oz butter
2 garlic cloves, chopped
250 g/9 oz mixed seafood, preferably raw, such as prawns, squid, mussels and clams
2 tbsp chopped oregano
50 g/1¾ oz freshly grated pecorino or Parmesan cheese

1 Place the stock in a large saucepan and bring to the boil over a medium heat. Add the rice and cook for about 12 minutes, stirring, until the rice is tender. Drain thoroughly, reserving any excess liquid.

2 Heat the butter in a large frying pan over a low heat. Add the garlic and stir.

3 Add the raw mixed seafood to the frying pan and cook for 5 minutes. If the seafood is already cooked, fry for 2–3 minutes.

4 Stir the chopped oregano into the seafood mixture in the frying pan.

5 Add the cooked rice to the pan and cook for 2–3 minutes, stirring, until hot. Add the reserved stock if the mixture gets too sticky. Add the grated cheese and mix well.

6 Transfer the risotto to 4 warmed serving dishes and serve immediately.

NUTRITION
Calories *679*; Sugars *8.9 g*; Protein *20.7 g*;
Carbohydrate *4.7 g*; Fat *15.8 g*; Saturates *1 g*

  easy

10 mins

25 mins

🍳 **COOK'S TIP**

The Genoese are excellent cooks, and they make particularly delicious fish dishes flavoured with the local olive oil.

Distinctive-tasting wild mushrooms, so popular in Italy, give this aromatic risotto a wonderful and robust flavour.

Wild Mushroom Risotto

1 Place the dried mushrooms in a bowl and pour over enough boiling water to cover. Leave to soak for 30 minutes, then carefully lift out and pat dry. Strain the soaking liquid through a sieve lined with kitchen paper and reserve.

2 Trim the wild mushrooms and gently brush clean.

3 Heat 3 tablespoons of the oil in a frying pan over a low heat. Add the fresh mushrooms and fry for 1–2 minutes. Add the garlic and soaked mushrooms and cook, stirring frequently, for 2 minutes. Transfer to a plate and reserve.

4 Heat the remaining olive oil and half the butter in a large saucepan over a low heat. Add the onion and cook, stirring occasionally, for 2 minutes, or until softened. Add the rice and cook, stirring frequently until translucent and well coated.   Add the vermouth. When almost absorbed, add a ladleful (about 225 ml/8 fl oz) of the stock. Cook, stirring, until the liquid is absorbed.

5 Continue adding the stock, about half a ladleful at a time, allowing each addition to be completely absorbed before adding the next. This should take 20–25 minutes. The risotto should have a creamy consistency and the rice should be tender, but still firm to the bite.

6 Add half the reserved mushroom soaking liquid to the risotto and stir in the mushrooms. Season to taste with salt and pepper and add more mushroom liquid, if necessary. Remove from the heat and stir in the remaining butter, the Parmesan cheese and chopped parsley. Transfer to 6 warmed serving dishes, garnish with parsley sprigs and serve with bread.

SERVES 6

55 g/2 oz dried porcini or morel mushrooms
about 500 g/1 lb 2 oz mixed fresh wild mushrooms, such as porcini, girolles, horse mushrooms and chanterelles, halved if large
4 tbsp olive oil
3–4 garlic cloves, chopped finely
4 tbsp unsalted butter
1 onion, chopped finely
350 g/12 oz arborio or carnaroli rice, rinsed
50 ml/2 fl oz dry white vermouth
1.2 litres/2 pints chicken stock, simmering
115 g/4 oz freshly grated Parmesan cheese
4 tbsp chopped fresh-flat leaf parsley
salt and pepper
6 fresh parsley sprigs, to garnish
crusty bread, to serve

NUTRITION
Calories 425; Sugars 2 g; Protein 16 g; Carbohydrate 54 g; Fat 17 g; Saturates 6 g

⭐⭐ easy

🕐 35 mins

🕐 35 mins

Try this combination of two types of rice with the richness of pine kernels, basil and freshly grated Parmesan cheese.

Pesto Rice *with* Garlic Bread

SERVES 4

300 g/10½ oz mixed long-grain and wild rice
4 fresh basil sprigs, to garnish
tomato and orange salad, to serve

pesto dressing
15 g/½ oz fresh basil sprigs
125 g/4½ oz pine kernels
2 garlic cloves, crushed
6 tbsp olive oil
55 g/2 oz freshly grated Parmesan cheese
salt and pepper

garlic bread
2 small granary or wholemeal French bread sticks
85 g/3 oz butter or margarine, softened
2 garlic cloves, crushed
1 tsp dried mixed herbs

1 Place the rice in a saucepan and cover with water. Bring to the boil over a medium heat and cook for 15–20 minutes. Drain thoroughly and keep warm.

2 Meanwhile, to make the pesto dressing. Remove the basil leaves from the stalks and finely chop the leaves. Reserve 25 g/1 oz of the pine kernels and finely chop the remainder. Mix with the chopped basil and the rest of the dressing ingredients. Alternatively, place all the ingredients in a food processor or blender and process for a few seconds until smooth. Reserve.

3 To make the garlic bread, slice the bread at 2.5 cm/1 inch intervals, taking care not to slice all the way through. Mix the butter or margarine with the garlic and mixed herbs. Season to taste with salt and pepper. Spread thickly between each slice. Wrap the bread in tinfoil and bake in a preheated oven at 200°C/400°F/Gas Mark 6, for 10–15 minutes.

4 To serve, toast the reserved pine kernels under a preheated medium-hot grill for 2–3 minutes until golden. Toss the pesto dressing into the hot rice and pile into 4 warmed serving dishes. Sprinkle with toasted pine kernels and garnish with a few basil sprigs. Serve with the garlic bread and a tomato and orange salad.

NUTRITION

Calories *918*; Sugars *2 g*; Protein *18 g*;
Carbohydrate *73 g*; Fat *64 g*; Saturates *19 g*

moderate

20 mins

40 mins

This traditional Easter risotto pie is from the Piedmont region in northern Italy. Serve it warm or chilled in slices.

Green Easter Pie

1 Lightly grease a 23-cm/9-inch deep cake tin with the butter and line the base with baking paper.

2 Using a sharp knife, roughly chop the rocket.

3 Heat the olive oil in a frying pan over a low heat. Add the onion and garlic and fry for 4–5 minutes, or until softened.

4 Add the rice to the frying pan, mix well, then start adding the stock a ladleful at a time. Allow each addition to be completely absorbed before adding the next.

5 Cook the mixture, adding the wine, until the rice is tender. This will take at least 20 minutes. Remove the pan from the heat.

6 Stir in the Parmesan cheese, peas, rocket, tomatoes, eggs and 2 tablespoons of the marjoram. Season to taste with salt and pepper.

7 Spoon the risotto into the prepared tin and level the surface by pressing down with the back of a wooden spoon. Top with the breadcrumbs and the remaining marjoram.

8 Bake in a preheated oven at 180°C/ 350°F/Gas Mark 4, for 30 minutes, or until set. Cut into slices and serve immediately.

SERVES 4

1 tbsp butter for greasing
85 g/3 oz rocket
2 tbsp olive oil
1 onion, chopped
2 garlic cloves, chopped
200 g/7 oz arborio rice, rinsed
700 ml/1¼ pints hot chicken or
   vegetable stock
125 ml/4 fl oz white wine
55 g/2 oz freshly grated Parmesan cheese
115 g/4 oz frozen peas, thawed
2 tomatoes, diced
4 eggs, beaten
3 tbsp fresh marjoram, chopped
55 g/2 oz fresh breadcrumbs
salt and pepper

NUTRITION
Calories *392*; Sugars *3 g*; Protein *17 g*;
Carbohydrate *41 g*; Fat *17 g*; Saturates *5 g*

moderate

25 mins

50 mins

Polenta is used in Italy in the same way as potatoes and rice. It has little flavour, but combined with butter, garlic and herbs, it is completely transformed.

Chilli Polenta Chips

SERVES 4

1.5 litres/2³⁄₄ pints water
350 g/12 oz instant polenta
2 tsp chilli powder
1 tbsp olive oil or melted butter
150 ml/5 fl oz soured cream
1 tbsp chopped fresh parsley
salt and pepper

1 Place the water in a large saucepan and bring to the boil over a medium heat. Add 2 teaspoons of salt, then add the polenta in a steady stream, stirring constantly.

2 Reduce the heat slightly and continue stirring for about 5 minutes. It is essential to stir the polenta, otherwise it will stick and burn. The polenta should have a thick consistency at this point and should be stiff enough to hold the spoon upright in the saucepan.

3 Add the chilli powder to the polenta mixture and stir well. Season to taste with a little salt and pepper.

4 Spread the polenta out on to a board or baking tray to about 4-cm/1½-inch thick. Leave to cool and set.

5 Cut the cooled polenta mixture into thin wedges.

6 Heat the olive oil in a frying pan over a medium heat. Add the polenta wedges and fry for 3–4 minutes on each side, or until golden and crispy. Alternatively, brush with melted butter and cook under a preheated hot grill for 6–7 minutes, or until golden. Drain the cooked polenta on kitchen paper.

7 Mix the soured cream with parsley and place in a bowl.

8 Transfer the polenta to a large serving plate and serve immediately with the soured cream and parsley dip.

NUTRITION
Calories 365; Sugars 1 g; Protein 8 g;
Carbohydrate 54 g; Fat 12 g; Saturates 5 g

easy

5 mins

20 mins

Here, skewers of thyme-flavoured polenta, wrapped in Parma ham, are grilled or barbecued.

Polenta Skewers *with* Parma Ham

1 Place the water in a large saucepan and bring to the boil over a medium heat. Add 2 teaspoons of salt, then add the polenta in a steady stream, stirring constantly. Reduce the heat slightly and continue stirring for about 5 minutes. It is essential to stir the polenta, otherwise it will stick and burn. The polenta should have a thick consistency at this point and should be stiff enough to hold the spoon upright in the saucepan.

2 Add the fresh thyme leaves to the polenta mixture and season to taste with salt and pepper. Spread out the polenta, about 2.5-cm/1-inch thick, on to a board, then leave to cool.

3 Using a sharp knife, cut the cooled polenta into 2.5-cm/1-inch cubes.

4 Cut the Parma ham slices into 2 pieces lengthways. Wrap the Parma ham around the polenta cubes.

5 Thread the wrapped polenta cubes on to presoaked wooden skewers.

6 Brush the kebabs with a little olive oil and cook under a preheated hot grill, turning frequently, for 7–8 minutes. Alternatively, barbecue the kebabs until golden. Transfer to 4 serving plates and serve with a green salad.

SERVES 4

175 g/6 oz instant polenta
700 ml/1¼ pints water
2 tbsp fresh thyme, stalks removed
8 slices Parma ham (about 75 g/2¾ oz)
1 tbsp olive oil
salt and pepper
fresh green salad, to serve

NUTRITION

Calories *213*; Sugars *27 g*; Protein *34 g*; Carbohydrate *3.2 g*; Fat *7.6 g*; Saturates *4 g*

 easy
 5 mins
🕐 20 mins

🍳 **COOK'S TIP**

Try flavouring the polenta with chopped oregano, basil or marjoram instead of the thyme, if you prefer. You should use 1½ tablespoons of chopped herbs to every 175 g/6 oz instant polenta.

These little potato dumplings are a traditional Italian appetiser but, served with a salad and bread, they make a substantial main course.

Gnocchi *with* Herb Sauce

SERVES 6

1 kg/2 lb 4 oz floury potatoes, cut into
   1-cm/½-inch pieces
55 g/2 oz butter or margarine
1 egg, beaten
300 g/10½ oz plain flour
salt and pepper

herb sauce
125 ml/4 fl oz olive oil
2 garlic cloves, very finely chopped
1 tbsp chopped fresh oregano
1 tbsp chopped fresh basil

to serve
freshly grated Parmesan cheese, optional
mixed salad
warm ciabatta bread

NUTRITION
Calories *619*; Sugars *3 g*; Protein *11 g*;
Carbohydrate *81 g*; Fat *30 g*; Saturates *9 g*

    moderate

🕐   30 mins

🕐   30 mins

1 Bring a large saucepan of lightly salted water to the boil over a medium heat. Add the potatoes and cook for 10 minutes, or until tender. Drain well.

2 Press the hot potatoes through a sieve into a large bowl. Add 1 teaspoon of salt, the butter or margarine, the egg and 150 g/5½ oz of the flour. Stir the mixture well to bind together.

3 Turn on to a lightly floured surface and knead, gradually adding the remaining flour, until a smooth, soft, slightly sticky dough is formed.

4 Flour your hands and roll the dough into 2-cm/¾-inch thick rolls. Cut each roll into 1-cm/½-inch pieces. Press the top of each piece with the floured prongs of a fork and spread out on a lightly floured tea towel.

5 Bring a large saucepan of lightly salted water to a gentle simmer over a low heat. Add the gnocchi and cook, in batches, for about 2–3 minutes, or until they rise to the surface.

6 Remove the gnocchi with a slotted spoon and place in a warmed, greased serving dish. Cover and keep warm.

7 To make the sauce, place the olive oil, garlic and seasoning in a saucepan and cook, stirring, for 3–4 minutes, or until the garlic is golden. Remove from the heat and stir in the herbs. Pour over the gnocchi and serve, sprinkled with grated Parmesan cheese and accompanied by salad and ciabatta.

Try not to handle the mixture too much when making gnocchi, as this will make the dough heavy.

Spinach *and* Ricotta Gnocchi

1 Wash and drain the spinach well. Cook in a covered saucepan without any extra liquid until softened, about 4 minutes, then place the spinach in a colander and press well to remove as much liquid as possible. Transfer the spinach to a blender and process until smooth. Alternatively, rub through a sieve.

2 Mix the spinach purée with the ricotta, half the pecorino cheese, the eggs and nutmeg. Season to taste with salt and pepper, then mix lightly but thoroughly. Work in enough flour, lightly and quickly, to make the mixture easy to handle.

3 Shape the dough quickly into small oval shapes, and dust lightly with flour.

4 Add 1 teaspoon of olive oil to a large saucepan of lightly salted water and bring to the boil over a medium heat. Add the gnocchi carefully and boil for 2 minutes, or until they rise to the surface. Using a slotted spoon, transfer the gnocchi to a buttered ovenproof dish and keep warm.

5 Melt the butter in a frying pan over a low heat. Add the pine kernels and raisins and fry until the nuts start to brown slightly, but do not allow the butter to burn.

6 Transfer the gnocchi to 4 warmed serving plates, pour the sauce over and sprinkle with the remaining grated pecorino cheese. Serve.

SERVES 4

1 kg/2 lb 4 oz fresh spinach leaves
350 g/12 oz ricotta cheese
125 g/4½ oz freshly grated pecorino cheese
3 eggs, beaten
¼ tsp freshly grated nutmeg
plain flour, to mix
1 tsp olive oil
125 g/4½ oz unsalted butter, plus extra
    for greasing
25 g/1 oz pine kernels
55 g/2 oz raisins
salt and pepper

NUTRITION
Calories 712; Sugars 15 g; Protein 28 g;
Carbohydrate 16 g; Fat 59 g; Saturates 33 g

      moderate

🕐   20 mins

🕐   15 mins

Semolina has a similar texture to polenta, but is slightly grainier. These gnocchi, which are flavoured with cheese and thyme, are easy to make.

Baked Semolina Gnocchi

SERVES 4

425 ml/15 fl oz vegetable stock
100 g/3½ oz semolina
1 tbsp fresh thyme, stalks removed
1 egg, beaten
50 g/1¾ oz freshly grated Parmesan cheese
50 g/1¾ oz butter, plus extra for greasing
2 garlic cloves, crushed
salt and pepper

1 Place the stock in a large saucepan and bring to the boil over a medium heat. Add the semolina in a steady trickle, stirring constantly. Keep stirring for 3–4 minutes, or until the mixture is thick enough to hold a spoon upright. Leave to cool slightly.

2 Add the thyme leaves, egg and half the cheese to the semolina mixture, and season to taste with salt and pepper.

3 Spread the semolina mixture on a board to a thickness of about 1 cm/ ½ inch, and leave until it has cooled and set.

4 When the semolina is completely cold, cut it into 2.5-cm/1-inch squares, reserving any offcuts.

5 Grease an ovenproof dish, placing the offcuts in the base. Arrange the semolina squares on top and sprinkle with the remaining cheese.

6 Melt the butter in a saucepan over a low heat. Add the garlic and season with pepper to taste. Pour the butter mixture over the gnocchi. Bake in a preheated oven at 220°C/425°F/Gas Mark 7, for 15–20 minutes, or until the gnocchi are puffed up and golden. Serve immediately.

NUTRITION
Calories 259; Sugars 0 g; Protein 9 g;
Carbohydrate 20 g; Fat 16 g; Saturates 10 g

⭐⭐   easy

🕑   15 mins

🕐   30 mins

👨‍🍳 **COOK'S TIP**

Try adding ½ tablespoon sun-dried tomato paste or 50 g/1¾ oz finely chopped mushrooms, fried in butter, to the semolina mixture in step 2. Follow the same cooking method.

Potatoes are used to make a 'pasta' dough, which is cut into noodles, boiled and served with a creamy bacon and mushroom sauce.

Noodles *with* Cheese Sauce

1 Bring a large saucepan of water to the boil over a medium heat. Add the potatoes and cook for 10 minutes, or until cooked through. Drain well. Mash the potatoes until smooth, then beat in the flour, egg and milk. Season to taste with salt and pepper, then bring together to form a stiff dough.

2 On a lightly floured surface, roll out the dough to form a thin sausage shape. Cut the sausage into 2.5-cm/1-inch lengths. Bring a large saucepan of lightly salted water to the boil over a medium heat. Drop in the dough pieces and cook for 3–4 minutes. They will rise to the surface when cooked.

3 To make the sauce, heat the vegetable oil in a frying pan over a low heat. Add the onion and garlic and sauté for 2 minutes. Add the mushrooms and bacon and cook for 5 minutes. Stir in the cheese, cream and parsley. Season to taste with salt and pepper.

4 Drain the noodles and transfer to a warmed serving bowl. Spoon the sauce over the top and toss to mix. Garnish with a parsley sprig and serve.

SERVES 4

450 g/1 lb floury potatoes, peeled and diced
225 g/8 oz plain flour
1 egg, beaten
1 tbsp milk
salt and pepper
1 fresh parsley sprig, to garnish

sauce
1 tbsp vegetable oil
1 onion, chopped
1 garlic clove, crushed
125 g/4½ oz open-cap mushrooms, sliced
3 smoked bacon slices, chopped
50 g/1¾ oz freshly grated Parmesan cheese
300 ml/10 fl oz double cream
2 tbsp chopped fresh parsley

NUTRITION
Calories 213; Sugars 1.6 g; Protein 5 g;
Carbohydrate 19 g; Fat 13 g; Saturates 7 g

⭐⭐   easy
🕐   5 mins
🕐   20 mins

 COOK'S TIP

Make the dough in advance, then wrap and store the noodles in the refrigerator for up to 24 hours.

Puddings *and* Desserts

For many people the favourite part of any meal is the dessert. The recipes that have been selected here will be a treat for all palates. Whether you are a chocolate lover or on a diet, in this chapter there is a recipe to tempt you. Choose from a light summer delicacy or a hearty hot winter treat – you will find desserts to indulge in all year round. If you are looking for a chilled sweet, choose the Rich Vanilla Ice Cream, or if a warm pudding takes your fancy, Crispy-Topped Fruit Bake will do the trick.

This melt-in-the-mouth version of a favourite cake has a fraction of the fat of the traditional version.

Carrot *and* Ginger Cake

SERVES 10

1 tbsp butter for greasing
225 g/8 oz plain flour
1 tsp baking powder
1 tsp bicarbonate of soda
2 tsp ground ginger
½ tsp salt
175 g/6 oz light muscovado sugar
225 g/8 oz carrots, grated
2 pieces chopped stem ginger
25 g/1 oz grated fresh root ginger
55 g/2 oz seedless raisins
2 medium eggs, beaten
3 tbsp corn oil
juice of 1 orange

frosting
225 g/8 oz low-fat soft cheese
4 tbsp icing sugar
1 tsp vanilla essence

to decorate
grated carrot
stem ginger, finely chopped and ground

NUTRITION
Calories *249*; Sugars *28 g*; Protein *7 g*;
Carbohydrate *46 g*; Fat *6 g*; Saturates *1 g*

moderate

15 mins

1 hr 15 mins

1 Grease and line a 20-cm/8-inch round cake tin with baking paper.

2 Sift the flour, baking powder, bicarbonate of soda, ground ginger and salt into a large mixing bowl. Stir in the sugar, carrots, stem ginger, fresh ginger and raisins. Beat the eggs, oil and orange juice together, then pour into the bowl. Mix the ingredients together well.

3 Spoon the mixture into the prepared tin and bake in the preheated oven at 180°C/350°F/Gas Mark 4, for 1–1¹/₄ hours, or until firm to the touch and a fine skewer inserted into the centre of the cake comes out clean. Leave to cool in the tin.

4 To make the frosting, place the soft cheese in a bowl and, using a wooden spoon, beat to soften. Sift in the icing sugar and add the vanilla essence. Mix well.

5 Remove the cake from the tin and smooth the frosting over the top. Decorate the cake with some grated carrot and ground stem ginger. Serve.

The sugar cubes give a lovely crunchy topping to this easy blackberry and apple dessert.

A substantial cake that is ideal for tea. The mashed bananas help to keep the cake moist and the lime icing gives it extra zing and zest.

Banana *and* Lime Cake

SERVES 10

1 tbsp butter for greasing
300 g/10½ oz plain flour
1 tsp salt
1½ tsp baking powder
175 g/6 oz light muscovado sugar
1 tsp grated lime rind
1 egg, beaten
1 banana, mashed with 1 tbsp lime juice
150 ml/5 fl oz low-fat natural fromage frais
115 g/4 oz sultanas

topping
115 g/4 oz icing sugar
1–2 tsp lime juice
½ tsp finely grated lime rind

to decorate
banana chips
finely grated lime rind

1 Grease and line a deep 18-cm/7-inch round cake tin with baking paper.

2 Sift the flour, salt and baking powder into a large mixing bowl and stir in the sugar and lime rind.

3 Make a well in the centre of the dry ingredients and add the egg, banana, fromage frais and sultanas. Mix well until thoroughly incorporated.

4 Spoon the mixture into the prepared tin and level the surface. Bake in a preheated oven at 180°C/350°F/Gas Mark 4, for 40–45 minutes, or until firm to the touch and a fine skewer inserted into the centre comes out clean.

5 Leave the cake to cool in the tin for 10 minutes, then turn out on to a wire rack to cool completely.

6 To make the topping, sift the icing sugar into a small bowl and mix with the lime juice to form a soft, but not too runny icing. Stir in the grated lime rind. Drizzle the icing over the cake, letting it run down the sides.

7 Decorate the cake with banana chips and lime rind. Leave the cake to stand for 15 minutes to allow the icing to set. Serve.

NUTRITION
Calories *235*; Sugars *31 g*; Protein *5 g*;
Carbohydrate *55 g*; Fat *1 g*; Saturates *0.3 g*

easy

35 mins

45 mins

Making these scones with mashed potato gives them a different texture from traditional scones, but they are just as delicious.

Potato *and* Nutmeg Scones

1 Grease and line a flat baking sheet or Swiss roll tin with baking paper.

2 Bring a large saucepan of unsalted water to the boil over a medium heat. Add the potatoes and cook for 10 minutes, or until softened. Drain, then using a potato masher, mash the potatoes.

3 Transfer the mashed potatoes to a large mixing bowl and stir in the flour, baking powder and freshly grated nutmeg, mixing well to blend the ingredients thoroughly.

4 Stir in the sultanas, egg and cream and, using a wooden spoon, beat the mixture until smooth.

5 Shape the mixture into 8 rounds, approximately 2-cm/³⁄₄-inch thick and place on the prepared baking sheet or Swiss roll tin.

6 Cook in a preheated oven at 200°C/ 400°F/Gas Mark 6, for 15 minutes, or until the scones have risen and are golden. Sprinkle the scones with the sugar and serve warm, spread with butter, if you wish.

SERVES 4

1 tbsp butter for greasing
225 g/8 oz floury potatoes, peeled and diced
125 g/4½ oz plain flour
1½ tsp baking powder
½ tsp freshly grated nutmeg
50 g/1¾ oz sultanas
1 egg, beaten
3 tbsp double cream
2 tsp soft light brown sugar

NUTRITION
Calories *135*; Sugars *6 g*; Protein *3 g*;
Carbohydrate *23 g*; Fat *4 g*; Saturates *2 g*

easy

5 mins

25 mins

COOK'S TIP

For convenience, make a batch of scones in advance and freeze them. Thaw thoroughly and warm in a preheated medium-hot oven when ready to serve.

This well-known dish is a light but rich mousse flavoured with Marsala. This dessert will not keep, so make it fresh and serve immediately.

Zabaglione

SERVES 4

5 egg yolks
100 g/3½ oz caster sugar
150 ml/5 fl oz Marsala wine or sweet sherry
amaretti biscuits, to serve (optional)

1 Place the egg yolks in a large mixing bowl.

2 Add the caster sugar and, using a balloon whisk, whisk together until the mixture is thick and very pale and has doubled in volume.

3 Place the bowl containing the whisked egg yolks and sugar over a saucepan of gently simmering water.

4 Add the Marsala wine or sherry to the egg yolk and sugar mixture and continue whisking until the foam mixture becomes warm. This process may take as long as 10 minutes.

5 Pour the mixture, which should be frothy and light, into 4 tall wine glasses.

6 Serve the zabaglione warm with amaretti biscuits, if you wish.

NUTRITION

Calories *158*; Sugars *29 g*; Protein *1 g*;
Carbohydrate *29 g*; Fat *1 g*; Saturates *0.2 g*

easy

15 mins

10 mins

🍳 COOK'S TIP

Any other type of liqueur may be used instead of the Marsala, or sweet sherry, if you prefer. Serve soft fruits such as strawberries or raspberries with the zabaglione – to make a delicious combination.

As this recipe only uses a little chocolate, choose one with a minimum of 70 per cent cocoa solids for a really good flavour.

Chocolate Zabaglione

1 Place the egg yolks and caster sugar in a large glass bowl and, using an electric whisk, whisk together until the mixture is very pale.

2 Grate the chocolate finely and fold into the egg mixture.

3 Fold the Marsala wine into the chocolate mixture.

4 Place the mixing bowl over a saucepan of gently simmering water and set the electric whisk on the lowest speed or swap to a balloon whisk. Cook gently, whisking constantly, until the mixture thickens. Take care not to overcook or the mixture will curdle.

5 Spoon the hot mixture into warmed individual glass dishes or coffee cups and serve the Zabaglione as soon as possible, while it is warm, light and fluffy, accompanied by amaretti biscuits.

SERVES 4

4 egg yolks
4 tbsp caster sugar
50 g/1¾ oz dark chocolate
125 ml/4 fl oz Marsala wine
amaretti biscuits, to serve

NUTRITION

Calories *227*; Sugars *29 g*; Protein *19 g*; Carbohydrate *29 g*; Fat *9.3 g*; Saturates *0.4 g*

⭐⭐　　easy
🕐　　10 mins
🕐　　5 mins

 COOK'S TIP

Make the dessert just before serving as it will separate if left to stand. If it starts to curdle, remove from the heat immediately and place it in a bowl of cold water. Whisk furiously until the mixture comes together.

This quick version of one of the most popular Italian desserts is ready in a matter of minutes.

Quick Tiramisù

SERVES 4

225 g/8 oz mascarpone or full-fat
  soft cheese
1 egg, separated
2 tbsp natural yogurt
2 tbsp caster sugar
2 tbsp dark rum
2 tbsp strong black coffee
8 sponge finger biscuits
2 tbsp grated dark chocolate

1 Place the cheese in a large mixing bowl, add the egg yolk and yogurt and, using a wooden spoon, beat until smooth.

2 Using a whisk, whisk the egg white in a separate spotlessly clean greasefree bowl until stiff but not dry, then whisk in the sugar and carefully fold into the cheese mixture.

3 Spoon half of the mixture into 4 tall sundae glasses.

4 Mix the rum and coffee together in a shallow dish. Dip the sponge finger biscuits into the rum mixture, break them in half or into smaller pieces, if necessary, and divide among the glasses.

5 Stir any of the remaining rum and coffee mixture into the remaining cheese and spoon over the top.

6 Sprinkle with grated chocolate and serve immediately. Alternatively, chill in the refrigerator until required.

NUTRITION
Calories *387*; Sugars *17 g*; Protein *9 g*; Carbohydrate *22 g*; Fat *28 g*; Saturates *15 g*

 moderate

15 mins

0 mins

 COOK'S TIP

Mascarpone is an Italian soft cream cheese made from cow's milk. It has a rich, silky smooth texture and a deliciously creamy flavour. It can be eaten as it is with fresh fruits or flavoured with coffee or chocolate.

This is the ultimate in self-indulgence – a truly delicious dessert that tastes every bit as good as it looks.

Raspberry Almond Spirals

1 Bring a large saucepan of lightly salted water to the boil over a medium heat. Add the pasta and cook until tender, but still firm to the bite. Drain the thoroughly, return to the pan and leave to cool.

2 Using the back of a spoon, firmly rub 225 g/8 oz of the raspberries through a sieve set over a large mixing bowl to form a smooth purée.

3 Put the raspberry purée and sugar in a small saucepan and simmer over a low heat, stirring occasionally, for 5 minutes. Stir in the lemon juice and leave the sauce until required.

4 Add the remaining raspberries to the fusilli in the pan and mix together well. Transfer the raspberry and fusilli mixture to a large serving dish.

5 Spread the almonds out on a baking tray and toast under a preheated hot grill until golden brown. Remove and leave to cool slightly.

6 Stir the raspberry liqueur into the reserved raspberry sauce and mix together well until very smooth. Pour the raspberry sauce over the fusilli, generously sprinkle over the toasted almonds and serve.

SERVES 4

175 g/6 oz dried fusilli
700 g/1 lb 9 oz fresh raspberries
2 tbsp caster sugar
1 tbsp lemon juice
4 tbsp flaked almonds
3 tbsp raspberry liqueur
salt

NUTRITION
Calories 235; Sugars 20 g; Protein 7 g;
Carbohydrate 36 g; Fat 7 g; Saturates 1 g

⭐⭐ easy
🕐 5 mins
🕐 20 mins

 COOK'S TIP

You could use almost any sweet, really ripe berry for making this dessert. Strawberries and blackberries are especially suitable, combined with the correspondingly flavoured liqueur.

If you prepare these in advance, all you have to do is pop the peaches on the barbecue when you are ready to serve them.

Peaches *with* Mascarpone

SERVES 4

4 firm but ripe fresh peaches
175 g/6 oz mascarpone cheese
40 g/1½ oz pecan nuts or walnuts, chopped
1 tsp sunflower oil
4 tbsp maple syrup

1 Cut the peaches in half and remove the stones. If you are preparing this recipe in advance, press the peach halves together and wrap in clingfilm.

2 Mix the mascarpone cheese and pecan nuts or walnuts together in a small bowl. Leave to chill in the refrigerator until required.

3 To serve, brush the peaches with a little sunflower oil and place on a rack set over medium-hot coals. Cook the peaches for 5–10 minutes, turning once, until hot.

4 Transfer the peaches to a serving dish and top them with the mascarpone cheese and nut mixture.

5 Drizzle maple syrup over the peaches and mascarpone cheese filling and serve immediately.

NUTRITION

Calories *301*; Sugars *24 g*; Protein *6 g*;
Carbohydrate *24 g*; Fat *20 g*; Saturates *9 g*

 very easy

🕐 10 mins

🕐 10 mins

🍳 **COOK'S TIP**

You can use nectarines instead of peaches. Remember to choose ripe but firm fruit, which won't go soft and mushy when it is barbecued. Prepare the nectarines in the same way as the peaches and barbecue for 5–10 minutes.

Italy is synonymous with ice cream. This home-made version of real vanilla ice cream is absolutely delicious and extremely easy to make.

Rich Vanilla Ice Cream

1 Place the cream in a heavy-based saucepan and heat gently over a low heat, whisking constantly. Add the vanilla pod, lemon rind, eggs and egg yolks, then heat until the mixture reaches just below boiling point.

2 Reduce the heat and cook for about 8–10 minutes, whisking the mixture constantly, until thickened.

3 Stir the sugar into the cream mixture and leave to cool.

4 Strain the cream mixture into a large bowl through a sieve.

5 Slit the vanilla pod open and scoop out the tiny black seeds. Stir them into the cream.

6 Pour the ice cream mixture into a shallow freezing container and freeze for 1 hour, then remove from the freezer and beat to break up the ice crystals. Return to the freezer and continue freezing. Repeat beating and freezing several times. Cover with a lid and store in the freezer until required. Transfer to the refrigerator just before serving to soften it slightly.

SERVES 4

600 ml/1 pint double cream
1 vanilla pod
pared rind of 1 lemon
4 eggs, beaten
2 egg yolks
175 g/6 oz caster sugar

NUTRITION
Calories *652*; Sugars *33 g*; Protein *8 g*;
Carbohydrate *33 g*; Fat *55 g*; Saturates *32 g*

⭐⭐ easy

🌀 5 mins

🕐 10 mins

 COOK'S TIP

Ice cream is one of the traditional dishes of Italy. Everyone eats it and there are numerous *gelato* stalls selling a wide variety of flavours, usually in a cone. It is also served in scoops, and even sliced!

These luxury biscuits will be popular at any time of the year, but make a particularly wonderful treat at Christmas.

Florentines

MAKES 10

4 tbsp butter
4 tbsp caster sugar
3 tbsp plain flour, sifted
50 g/1¾ oz almonds, chopped
50 g/1¾ oz chopped mixed peel
25 g/1 oz raisins, chopped
25 g/1 oz glacé cherries, chopped
finely grated rind of ½ lemon
125 g/4½ oz dark chocolate, melted

1 Line 2 large baking trays with baking paper.

2 Heat the butter and caster sugar in a small saucepan over a low heat until the butter has just melted and the sugar dissolved. Remove the pan from the heat.

3 Stir in the flour and mix well. Stir in the chopped almonds, mixed peel, raisins, cherries and lemon rind. Place teaspoonfuls of the mixture well apart on the baking trays.

4 Bake in a preheated oven at 180°C/ 350°F/Gas Mark 4, for 10 minutes, or until lightly golden.

5 As soon as the florentines are removed from the oven, press the edges into neat shapes while still on the baking trays with a biscuit cutter. Leave to cool on the baking trays until firm, then transfer to a wire rack to cool completely.

6 Spread the melted chocolate over the smooth side of each florentine. As the chocolate begins to set, mark wavy lines in it with a fork. Leave the florentines until set, chocolate side up.

NUTRITION
Calories *164*; Sugars *20 g*; Protein *2.5 g*;
Carbohydrate *12.8 g*; Fat *10 g*; Saturates *7.5 g*

⭐⭐ easy
🕐 50 mins
🕐 10 mins

 COOK'S TIP

Replace the dark chocolate with white chocolate or, for a dramatic effect, cover half of the florentines in dark chocolate and half in white.

A wonderful mixture of summer fruits encased in slices of white bread, which soak up all the deep red, flavoursome juices.

Summer Puddings

1 Grease 6 150-ml/5-fl oz moulds with the butter or oil.

2 Line the moulds with the bread, cutting the slices to fit snugly.

3 Place the sugar in a small saucepan with the water and heat gently over a low heat, stirring frequently, until dissolved. Bring to the boil over a high heat and boil for 2 minutes.

4 Reserve 6 large strawberries for decoration. Add half the raspberries and the rest of the fruits to the syrup, cutting the strawberries in half if large, and simmer gently for a few minutes, until they are starting to soften but still retain their shape.

5 Spoon the fruits and some of the liquid into moulds. Cover with more slices of bread. Spoon a little juice around the sides of the moulds so the bread is well soaked. Cover with a saucer and a heavy weight, leave to cool, then chill thoroughly in the refrigerator, preferably overnight.

6 Place the remaining raspberries in a food processor or blender and process until smooth. Alternatively, rub the raspberries through a non-metallic sieve. Add a little extra liquid to the raspberries if necessary to give the sauce a coating consistency.

7 Invert on to 4 serving plates and spoon the raspberry sauce over. Decorate with a mint sprig and the reserved strawberries. Serve with cream.

SERVES 4

1 tbsp butter or vegetable oil for greasing
6–8 thin slices white bread, crusts removed
175 g/6 oz caster sugar
300 ml/10 fl oz water
225 g/8 oz strawberries
500 g/1 lb 2 oz raspberries
175 g/6 oz blackcurrants and/or redcurrants
175 g/6 oz blackberries or loganberries
4 fresh mint sprigs, to decorate
single cream, to serve

NUTRITION
Calories 250; Sugars 41 g; Protein 4 g; Carbohydrate 53 g; Fat 4 g; Saturates 2 g

 moderate
10 mins
10 mins

This famous Tuscan honey and nut cake is a Christmas speciality. In Italy it is sold in pretty boxes, and served in very thin slices.

Panforte *di* Siena

SERVES 4

125 g/4½ oz almonds, halved
125 g/4½ oz hazelnuts
85 g/3 oz chopped mixed peel
55 g/2 oz ready to eat dried apricots
55 g/2 oz glacé or crystallized pineapple
grated rind of 1 large orange
55 g/2 oz plain flour
2 tbsp cocoa powder
2 tsp ground cinnamon
125 g/4½ oz caster sugar
175 g/6 oz honey
sifted icing sugar, for dredging

NUTRITION
Calories 257; Sugars 29 g; Protein 5 g;
Carbohydrate 33 g; Fat 13 g; Saturates 1 g

moderate

10 mins

1 hr 15 mins

1 Place the almonds on a large baking tray and toast under a preheated hot grill until lightly browned. Place in a bowl.

2 Place the hazelnuts on a large baking tray and toast under the preheated hot grill until the skins split. Place on a dry tea towel and rub off the skins. Roughly chop the hazelnuts and add them to the almonds along with the mixed peel.

3 Chop the apricots and pineapple finely, then add to the nuts with the orange rind and mix well.

4 Sift the flour with the cocoa and cinnamon, add to the nut mixture; mix.

5 Line a round 20-cm/8-inch cake tin or deep loose-based flan tin with non-stick baking paper.

6 Put the sugar and honey into a saucepan and heat over a low heat until the sugar dissolves. Increase the heat and boil gently for about 5 minutes, or until the mixture thickens and starts to turn a deeper shade of brown. Quickly add to the nut mixture and stir well to mix evenly. Turn into the prepared tin and level the top using the back of a damp spoon.

7 Cook the cake in a preheated oven at 150°C/300°F/Gas Mark 2, for 1 hour. Remove from the oven and leave to cool in the tin until completely cold. Turn out of the tin and carefully peel off the paper. Before serving, dredge the cake heavily with sifted icing sugar and serve in very thin slices.

This cheesecake takes a little time to prepare and cook, but it is well worth the effort. It is quite rich and is good served with some fresh fruit, such as Cape gooseberries.

Chocolate Tofu Cheesecake

1 Place the flour, ground almonds and 1 tablespoon of the sugar in a large bowl and mix well. Rub the margarine into the mixture to form a dough.

2 Lightly grease and line the base of a 23-cm/9-inch springform tin with baking paper. Press the dough into the base of the tin, pushing the dough right up to the edge of the tin.

3 Roughly chop the tofu and place in a food processor with the vegetable oil, orange juice, brandy, cocoa powder, almond essence and remaining sugar, and process until smooth and creamy. Pour over the base in the tin and cook in a preheated oven at 160°C/325°F/Gas Mark 3, for about 1–1¼ hours, or until the tofu is set.

4 Leave to cool in the tin for 5 minutes, then remove from the tin and chill in the refrigerator. Dust with icing sugar and cocoa powder. Decorate with Cape gooseberries and serve.

SERVES 4

100 g/3½ oz plain flour
100 g/3½ oz ground almonds
200 g/7 oz muscovado sugar
150 g/5½ oz margarine
675 g/1 lb 8 oz firm tofu (drained weight)
175 ml/6 fl oz vegetable oil
125 ml/4 fl oz orange juice
175 ml/6 fl oz brandy
6 tbsp cocoa powder, plus extra to decorate
2 tsp almond essence

to decorate
icing sugar
Cape gooseberries

NUTRITION
Calories 471; Sugars 20 g; Protein 10 g;
Carbohydrate 28 g; Fat 33 g; Saturates 5 g

 moderate
1 hr 15 mins
1 hr 15 mins

COOK'S TIP

Cape gooseberries or physalis make a very attractive decoration for many desserts. Peel open the papery husks to expose the bright orange fruits.

Index

A

aromatic seafood rice 78
artichoke and olive spaghetti 135

B

bacon, bean and garlic soup 32
baked semolina gnocchi 156
bamboo shoots 12
banana and lime cake 162
basic recipes 14_15
bean sprouts 12
Béchamel sauce 14
beef
    chunky potato and beef soup 35
    creamed strips of sirloin 86
    meatballs in red wine sauce 89
    and pasta bake 88
    satay 60
    Sicilian spaghetti cake 87
beetroot and potato soup 39
black beans 12
bottled sauces 11
bread
    ciabatta rolls 53
    crostini alla Fiorentina 59
    garlic 150
    grilled chicken with pesto toasts 112
    hummus toasts with olives 47
    pork sesame toasts 56
    potato and nutmeg scones 163
    Tuscan ciabatta 49
broccoli and asparagus gemelli 124
butterfly lamb with mint 97

C

cakes
    banana and lime 162
    carrot and ginger 160
    panforte di Siena 172
Calabrian mushroom soup 23
carrot and ginger cake 160
casseroles
    beans and penne 126
    rich chicken 105
cheese
    garlic and herb pâté 43
    pasta squares 145
    sauce 14, 157
chick-pea soup 22
chicken
    with balsamic vinegar 110
    cacciatora 113
    curried chicken soup 28
    garlic and herb 104
    with green olives 111
    and leek soup 30
    lemon conchiglie 114
    Marengo 115
    with orange sauce 108
    and pasta soup 29
    pepperonata 107
    with pesto toasts 112
    rich casserole 105
    satay 60
    sauce 106, 146
    sesame ginger 57
    skewered spirals 109
chillies 9
    fish soup 26
    polenta chips 152
    shrimp noodles 75
    tagliatelle 131
Chinese crab soup with ginger 27
Chinese ingredients
    beans 12
    five-spice powder 12
    leaves 12
chocolate
    tofu cheesecake 173
    zabaglione 165
chunky potato and beef soup 35
ciabatta rolls 53
citrus pork chops 92
cream sauce 91
creamy strips of sirloin 86
crispy dishes
    fruit bake 161
    golden seafood 51
    seaweed 54
crostini alla Fiorentina 59
curried chicken soup 28

D

delicately spiced trout 81
desserts 159–73
dips
    heavenly garlic 42
    tzatziki and black olive 46
dried fruits 9
duck with raspberry sauce 116

E

escalopes and Italian sausages 101
Espagnole sauce 15

F

fats 9
figs and Parma ham 50
fillets of red mullet and pasta 69
fish
    aromatic seafood rice 78
    chilli fish soup 26
    chilli shrimp noodles 75
    Chinese crab soup with ginger 27
    crispy golden seafood 51
    delicately spiced trout 81
    fillets of red mullet and pasta 69
    Indian cod with tomatoes 79
    lamb and anchovies with thyme 94
    mussel salad 65
    mussels in white wine 52
    noodles with cod and mango 76
    pasta and anchovy sauce 61
    pasta with clams and white wine 141
    plaice with mushrooms 80
    pork sesame toasts 56
    prawn pasta bake 72
    salmon steaks with penne 71
    seafood chow mein 73
    seafood salad 64
    smoked fish and potato pâté 44
    smoked haddock soup 31
    smoked trout and apple salad 67
    smoky fish skewers 82
    spaghetti and salmon sauce 139
    spaghetti and shellfish 140
    spicy salt and pepper prawns 58
    sweet and sour noodles 74
    sweet and sour tuna salad 66
    trout with smoked bacon 70
    tuna, bean and anchovy salad 68
five-spice powder 12
florentines 170
fusilli salad with chilli 136

G

gardener's broth 38
garlic
    bread 150
    cheese and herb pâté 43
    and herb chicken 104
    pork with lemon 93
    spaghetti 129
gnocchi
    baked semolina 156
    with herb sauce 154
    spinach and ricotta 155

grains 7
green Easter pie 151
grilled chicken with pesto toasts 112

H
heavenly garlic dip 42
herbs 9
    sauce 154
hoisin sauce 12
hummus toasts with olives 47

I
Indian cod with tomatoes 79
ingredients 7–13, 17
Italian dishes
    red wine sauce 15
    risotto 147
    tomato sauce and pasta 123

L
lamb
    and anchovies with thyme 94
    with bay and lemon 96
    cutlets with rosemary 95
    with mint 97
    and rice soup 25
lemon chicken conchiglie 114
lentil pâté 45
lime partridge with pesto 117
lychees 12

M
macaroni and corn pancakes 122
mango 12
meat 85–101
meatballs in red wine sauce 89
mixed seafood risotto 148
mushrooms
    Calabrian soup 23
    and ginger soup 36
    risotto 149
mussels
    salad 65
    in white wine 52
mustards 11

N
Neapolitan veal cutlets 99
noodles 12–13
    with cheese sauce 157
    chilli shrimp 75
    with cod and mango 76

oyster sauce 77
    sweet and sour 74
nutritional information 17
nuts 9

O
oils 9
orange sauce 108
oriental ingredients 12–13
oyster sauce 13
    noodles 77

P
pak choi 13
    crispy seaweed 54
panforte di Siena 172
partridge with pesto 117
pasta 7
    and anchovy sauce 61
    artichoke and olive spaghetti 135
    beef and pasta bake 88
    broccoli and asparagus gemelli 124
    casseroled beans and penne 126
    and cheese puddings 132
    cheesy squares 145
    with chicken sauce 106
    chicken soup 29
    chilli tagliatelle 131
    and chilli tomatoes 138
    with clams and white wine 141
    with classic pesto sauce 128
    fillets of red mullet 69
    fusilli salad with chilli 136
    with garlic and broccoli 125
    garlic spaghetti 129
    Italian tomato sauce 123
    lemon chicken conchiglie 114
    with nuts and cheese 137
    pasticcio 144
    penne and butternut squash 142
    and pork in cream sauce 91
    prawn bake 72
    salmon steaks with penne 71
    Sicilian spaghetti cake 87
    spaghetti Bolognese 120
    spaghetti with ricotta cheese 134
    spaghetti and shellfish 140
    tagliatelle and chicken sauce 146
    three-cheese macaroni 121
    tomato soup 24
    vegetable nests 143
    and vegetable sauce 127

    vegetables and tofu 130
    walnut and olive 133
pasticcio 144
pâtés
    cheese, garlic and herb 43
    lentils 45
    smoked fish and potato 44
peaches with mascarpone 168
penne and butternut squash 142
pepper salad 48
pesto
    rice with garlic bread 150
    sauce 128
plaice with mushrooms 80
polenta
    chilli chips 152
    skewers with Parma ham 153
    spicy sweetcorn fritters 55
pork
    chops with sage 90
    citrus pork chops 92
    with lemon and garlic 93
    pasta and pork in cream sauce 91
    sesame toasts 56
potatoes
    and beef soup 35
    beetroot soup 39
    and nutmeg scones 163
    smoked fish pâté 44
poultry 103–117
prawn pasta bake 72
prosciutto
    figs and Parma ham 50
    polenta skewers with Parma ham 153
puddings 159–73
pulses 9

Q
quick tiramisù 166

R
ragu sauce 15
raspberries
    almond spirals 167
    sauce 116
red mullet fillets and pasta 69
red wine sauce 15, 89
rice 7
    aromatic seafood 78
    green Easter pie 151
    Italian risotto 147

lamb and rice soup 25
mixed seafood risotto 148
pesto rice with garlic bread 150
vinegar 13
wild mushroom risotto 149
wine 13
rich dishes
chicken casserole 105
vanilla ice cream 169
rose petal sauce 98

S
salads
fusilli with chilli 136
mussels 65
pepper 48
seafood 64
smoked trout and apple 67
sweet and sour tuna 66
tuna, bean and anchovy 68
salmon
sauce 139
steaks with penne 71
sauces
basic 14–15
bottled 11
cheese 157
chicken 106, 146
cream 91
herb 154
Italian tomato 123
orange 108
pasta and anchovy 61
pasta and vegetable 127
pesto 128
raspberry 116
red wine 89
rose petal 98
salmon 139
scallop skewers 83
seafood 63–83
chow mein 73
risotto 148
salad 64
seeds 9
sesame oil 13
ginger chicken 57
Sicilian spaghetti cake 87
skewered chicken spirals 109
smoked fish
haddock soup 31
and potato pâté 44

skewers 82
trout and apple salad 67
snacks 41–61
soups
bacon, bean and garlic 32
beetroot and potato 39
Calabrian mushroom 23
chick-pea 22
chicken and leek 30
chicken and pasta 29
chilli fish 26
Chinese crab with ginger 27
chunky potato and beef 35
curried chicken 28
gardener's broth 38
lamb and rice 25
mushroom and ginger 36
smoked haddock 31
spicy dhal and carrot 33
spicy lentil 34
tomato and pasta 24
Tuscan onion 20
vegetable and bean 21
yogurt and spinach 37
soy sauce 13
spaghetti
Bolognese 120
garlic 129
with ricotta cheese 134
and salmon sauce 139
and shellfish 140
spices 11
spicy dishes
dhal and carrot soup 33
lentil soup 34
salt and pepper prawns 58
sweetcorn fritters 55
spinach and ricotta gnocchi 155
star anise 13
starters 41–61
summer puddings 171
sweet and sour dishes
noodles 74
tuna salad 66
Szechuan pepper 13

T
tagliatelle and chicken sauce 146
three-cheese macaroni 121
tips 17
tiramisu 166
tofu 13

chocolate tofu cheesecake 173
vegetables and tofu 130
tomatoes
and pasta soup 24
sauce 14, 123
trout
and apple salad 67
delicately spiced 81
with smoked bacon 70
tuna, bean and anchovy salad 68
Tuscan dishes
ciabatta 49
onion soup 20
tzatziki and black olive dips 46

V
vanilla ice cream 169
veal
Italienne 100
Neapolitan cutlets 99
in a rose petal sauce 98
vegetables
and bean soup 21
pasta nests 143
and tofu 130
vinegars 11, 13

W
walnut and olive pasta 133
water chestnuts 13
wild mushroom risotto 149

Y
yellow beans 13
yoghurt and spinach soup 37

Z
zabaglione 164
chocolate 165